CHRIS TURNER

LOOKING AT Criminal LAW

Hodder & Stoughton

A MEMBER OF THE HODDER HEADLINE GROUP

Orders: please contact Bookpoint Ltd, 130 Milton Park, Abingdon, Oxon OX14 4SB. Telephone: (44) 01235 827720.
Fax: (44) 01235 400454. Lines are open from 9.00 – 6.00, Monday to Saturday, with a 24 hour message answering service.
You can also order through our website: www.hodderheadline.co.uk

British Library Cataloguing in Publication Data

A catalogue record for this title is available from The British Library

ISBN 0 340 87167 9

First Published 2003

Impression number 10 9 8 7 6 5 4 3

Year 2007 2006

Copyright © 2003 Chris Turner

Typeset by **Dorchester Typesetting Group Limited**
Printed in India for Hodder & Stoughton Educational, a division of Hodder Headline Plc, 338 Euston Road, London
NW1 3BH by Replika Press Pvt. Ltd.

CONTENTS

This is the second book of resources and exercises. The first covered all substantive options from the major A Level boards: Criminal Law, Contract and Tort. That first edition was a companion to Jacqueline Martin's similar resource book on the *English Legal System* and the wider range of A Level texts. Since the introduction of the original *Substantive Law Resources Workbook*, teachers have asked both me and the editorial staff at Hodder on numerous occasions for an edition that focuses purely on resources and exercises in Criminal Law. Inevitably, two-thirds of the first edition were wasted to many students using it. Since Criminal Law has the most take-up at A Level Law, accounting for more than 70% of OCR candidates; for instance, then here it is. Again this book is aimed primarily at students on A Level Law courses, of whatever examining board, but there is no reason why it should not be used by any first-time student of Criminal Law.

The book retains all the features of the original, being made up of a variety of resources, materials, exercises and other learning aids. It is broken down into sections roughly representing the sorts of chapters that you will find in the textbooks, each of which is preceded by a brief overview of the area outlining the sorts of points that may be raised in the source material.

It can be a companion to Diana Roe's text on *Criminal Law* or could be used to supplement any textbook on Criminal Law.

The materials in the book include:

- extracts from the judgments of reported cases
- extracts from Acts of Parliament or from delegated legislation
- articles from newspapers, journals, and even reports of law reform bodies.

These extracts vary in size, but they are all edited to introduce the reader to actual primary sources of law but in manageable proportions.

They are all accompanied by questions to test comprehension of the material. Some questions require only brief answers; others are more thought-provoking, and also included are some questions that are similar to actual exam questions. There are also some exercises or activities that offer a more practical way of testing understanding. There are also a number of

activities of a much more lighthearted nature which have been moved from the back of the book to run alongside the actual chapters.

One chapter presents students with hints on revision exercises.

A new addition to the book is a chapter on the synoptic element of the A Level exams: the Special Study Paper. In the case of OCR I write and lead on this paper so it perhaps provides some insight into the nature of the paper and the expectations of the examiners.

The last chapter is again an examiner's view of how to cope with the different types of questions that you may come across during exams, whether it be traditional essay questions, problem solving or the more recent data response-type questions.

As with the original book, I hope that this is an accessible and lively alternative to other learning methods and that you will enjoy using it and also find it useful, and that you will enjoy your study of the law. I would repeat what I said at the end of the preface to the first edition: 'The law is ultimately about people and the often strange things that happen to them. All of the reported cases here involve real events, and as you read many of the reports you will realise the reality of the old maxim that the truth is stranger than fiction. Hopefully you will find also that the law is in fact as entertaining and interesting as any work of fiction.'

ACKNOWLEDGEMENTS

The author and the publishers would like to thank the following for permission to reproduce copyright material:

- Extracts reproduced by kind permission of *The Legal Executive Journal*
- © *The Times*
- Parliamentary copyright material from 'Violence: Reforming the Offences Against the Person Act, 1981, Draft Offences Against the Person Bill 1998' is reproduced with the permission of the Controller of Her Majesty's Stationery Office on behalf of Parliament
- *Justice of The Peace*
- *Criminal Law Review*
- Sweet & Maxwell for the extract from *Criminal Law Text and Materials* by CMV Clarkson and HM Keating (1998) p 632
- Butterworths Tolley for extracts from the *All England Reports* and from *New Law Journal*
- AQA examination questions are reproduced by permission of the Assessment and Qualifications Alliance
- OCR for use of examination questions

Every effort has been made to trace copyright holders but this has not always been possible in all cases; any omissions brought to our attention will be corrected in future printings.

CHAPTER 1

THE ELEMENTS OF A CRIME: *ACTUS REUS*

Most crimes require both conduct which is criminal and the necessary criminal intent. The conduct element and the circumstances surrounding it are known as the '*actus reus*'. The key aspects of the *actus reus* are that it should involve voluntary conduct, and that it should be the cause of the consequence which the law sees as unacceptable, and thus criminal. Sometimes an omission rather than a deed can be the *actus reus*. On rare occasions, a mere state of affairs is criminal.

Voluntary act

Extract adapted from the judgment in *Bratty v Attorney General for Northern Ireland* [1963] AC 386, HL

Facts

The appellant strangled a girl and claimed that at the time he was totally unaware of what he was doing. The trial judge refused to put his claim of non-insane automatism to the jury and the appellant was convicted. His eventual appeal to the House of Lords failed.

Judgment

LORD DENNING:
The requirement that [the act] should be a voluntary act is essential, not only in a murder case, but also in every criminal case. No act is punished if it is involuntary ...

The term 'involuntary act', however, is capable of wider connotations: ... in the criminal law an act is not to be regarded as an involuntary act simply because the doer does not remember it ... it is no defence to him to say 'I don't know what happened. I cannot remember a "thing," ': see *Hill v Baxter...* Nor is an act to be regarded as ... involuntary ... simply because the doer could not control his impulse to do it ... though it may go towards a defence of diminished responsibility ... see *R v Byrne* ... Nor is an act to be regarded as ... involuntary ... simply because it is unintentional or its consequences are unforeseen. Where a man is charged with dangerous driving it is no defence for him to say ... 'I did not mean to drive dangerously.' Nevertheless, he has a defence if he can show that it was an involuntary act in the sense that he was unconscious at the time and he did not know what he was doing.

State of affairs

Extract adapted from the judgment in *R v Larsonneur* [1933] 97 JP 206, Court of Criminal Appeal

Facts

Larsonneur, a French woman, landed in England with only a temporary stay on her passport. This was later revoked and she was required to leave by a certain date. She then went to Ireland where she was deported and transported back to England. She was arrested and charged with being in breach of the Aliens Order 1920. She had no choice about returning to England, and had no control over her presence here but she was still guilty of the offence.

Judgment

LORD HEWART CJ:
The appellant ... was at Holyhead on 21 April 1933, practically a month after the day limited by the condition on her passport.

In these circumstances it seems quite clear that the Aliens Order 1920 applies. The appellant was in the position she would have been if she had been prohibited from landing by the Secretary of State. She was found here and was, therefore, deemed to be in the class of persons whose landing had been prohibited by the Secretary of State, by reason of the fact that she had violated the condition on her passport.

Omissions

Extract adapted from the judgment in *R v Stone and Dobinson* [1977] 1 QB 354, CA

Facts

A very inadequate couple, a man aged 67, partially deaf, almost blind and of low intelligence, and a woman aged 43, and described as 'ineffectual', took into their home the woman's younger sister. She was suffering from anorexia nervosa. The couple were inadequate to look after her, failed at first to get her a doctor and eventually she died. They were convicted of manslaughter and appealed unsuccessfully.

Judgment

GEOFFREY LANE LJ:

There is no dispute as to the matters on which the jury must be satisfied before they can convict of manslaughter in circumstances such as the present. They are (1) that the defendant undertook the care of a person who by reason of age or infirmity was unable to care for himself; (2) that the defendant was grossly negligent in regard to his duty of care; (3) that by reason of such negligence the person died.

[Counsel for the appellants] submitted that the evidence that might support the assumption of a duty by the appellants does not, when examined, succeed in doing so. Fanny came to this house as a lodger. Largely if not entirely due to her own eccentricity and failure to look after herself or feed herself properly, she became increasingly infirm and immobile and eventually unable to look after herself. The suggestion is that, heartless though it may seem, this is one of those situations where the appellants were entitled to do nothing; where no duty was cast upon them to help, any more than it is cast upon a man to rescue a stranger from drowning, however easy such a rescue might be.

This was not a situation analogous [similar] to the drowning stranger. They did make efforts to care. They tried to get a doctor; they tried to discover the previous doctor. Dobson helped with the washing and the provision of food. All these matters were put before the jury in terms which we find it impossible to fault. They were entitled to find that the duty had been assumed. They were entitled to conclude that once Fanny became helplessly infirm the appellants were ... obliged either to summon help or else to care for Fanny themselves.

Extract adapted from the judgment in *R v Miller* [1983] 2 AC 161, HL

Facts

Miller was staying in a 'squat'. He fell asleep one night while smoking. He woke with his mattress burning but did nothing about it, but just moved to another room. The house caught fire and Miller was convicted of arson. His appeal, on the ground that the fire was started accidentally, without *mens rea*, and that he could not be convicted for omitting to put out the fire, failed.

Judgment

LORD DIPLOCK:

Since arson is a result-crime the period may be considerable, and during it the conduct of the accused that is causative of the result may consist not only of his doing physical acts which cause the fire to start or spread but also of his failing to take measures that lie within his power to counteract the danger that he has himself created.

1.4 Causation

Extract adapted from the judgment in *R v White* [1910] All ER Rep 340, Court of Criminal Appeal

Facts

White's mother had been found dead from a heart attack. She had nearby a drink that was found to contain potassium cyanide. There was no evidence to suggest that she had drunk any of the poison, which was in any case of insufficient quantity to cause her death. White was convicted of attempted murder and appealed unsuccessfully.

Judgment

BRAY J:

We are of opinion that there was sufficient evidence to warrant the jury coming to the conclusion that the appellant put the cyanide in the glass with intent to murder his mother.

The next point was made that, if he put it there with that intent there was no attempt at murder; he intended to cause her death by slow poisoning and there was no attempt at murder, because the act of which he was guilty – viz, the putting of poison in the glass – was a completed act and could not be and was not intended to have the effect of killing her at once. It could not kill unless it were followed by other acts which he might never have done. We are of opinion that the completion or attempted completion of one of a series of acts intended by a man to result in killing is an attempt to murder even though this completed act would not, unless followed by the other acts, result in killing.

Extract adapted from the judgment in *R v Blaue* [1975] 1 WLR 1411

Facts

Blaue stabbed a woman and perforated her lung. The woman was told that she needed a blood transfusion, but refused it because of her beliefs as a Jehovah's Witness, and she then died. The medical treatment would have saved the woman's life but Blaue was still convicted of murder and appealed, unsuccessfully, on the ground that there was a break in the chain of causation.

Judgment

LAWTON LJ:

Counsel for the defendant invited the judge to direct the jury to acquit. His argument was that her refusal to have a blood transfusion had broken the chain of causation between the stabbing and her death.

When the judge came to direct the jury on this issue he did so by telling them that they should apply their common sense. He then went on to tell them that they would get help from the cases to which counsel had referred. He placed particular reliance on what Maule J had said in *R v Holland*. He continued:

> 'This is one of those relatively rare cases, you may think, with very little option open to you but to reach the conclusion that was reached by your predecessors As members of the jury in *R v Holland*, namely, "yes" to the question of causation that the stab was still the operative cause of death – or a substantial cause of death. However, that is a matter for you to determine.'

In *R v Holland* Maule J said 'the real question is, whether in the end the wound inflicted by the prisoner was the cause of death.' That distinguished judge left the jury to decide that question as did the judge in this case. They had to decide it as juries always do, by pooling their experience of life and using their common sense.

Maule J's direction to the jury reflected the common law's answer to the problem. He who inflicted an injury which resulted in death could not excuse himself by pleading that his victim could have avoided death by taking greater care of himself.

Mr Comyn tried to overcome this line of reasoning by submitting that the jury should have been directed that if they thought the deceased's decision not to have a blood transfusion was an unreasonable one, then the chain of causation would have been broken. At once the question arises – reasonable by whose standards?

As was pointed out in the course of argument two cases, each raising the same issue of reasonableness because of religious beliefs, could produce different verdicts depending on where the cases were tried. Mr Comyn accepted that this might be so: it was, he said, inherent in trial by jury. It is not inherent in the common law as expounded by Maule J. It has long been the policy of the law that those who use violence on other people must take their victims as they find them. It does not lie in the mouth of the assailant to say that the victim's religious beliefs which inhibited him from accepting certain … treatment were unreasonable. The question for decision is what caused her death. The answer is the stab wound. The fact that the victim refused to stop this end coming about did not break the causal connection between the act and the death.

Extract from the judgment in *R v Pagett* (1983) 76 Cr App Rep 279, CA

Facts

The appellant abducted his girlfriend and held her hostage in a flat at gunpoint. When the flat was under siege by armed police the appellant used the girlfriend as a human shield when firing at police. The police fired back in self-defence and the girl was killed. Pagett appealed unsuccessfully against his conviction for manslaughter, on the ground that he had not caused the girl's death.

Judgment

ROBERT GOFF LJ:

In cases of homicide, it is rarely necessary to give the jury any direction on causation as such. Of course, a necessary ingredient of the crimes of murder and manslaughter is that the accused has by his act caused the victim's death ... Even where it is necessary to direct the jury's minds to the question of causation, it is usually enough to direct them simply that in law the accused's act need not be the sole cause, or even the main cause, of the victim's death, it being enough that his act contributed significantly to that result. It is right to observe in passing, however, that even this simple direction is a direction of law relating to causation, on the basis of which a jury are bound to act in concluding whether the prosecution has established, as a matter of fact, that the accused's act did in this sense cause the victim's death. Occasionally, however, a specific issue of causation may arise. One such case is where, although an act of the accused constitutes ... a necessary condition ... for the death of the accused, nevertheless the intervention of a third person may be regarded as the sole cause of the victim's death, thereby relieving the accused of criminal responsibility ... often described ... as *novus actus interveniens.*

[However, certain] examples of ... non-voluntary conduct [by third parties] is not effective to relieve the accused of responsibility ... two ... are germane to the present case, *viz*, a reasonable act performed for the purpose of self-preservation, and an act done in the performance of a legal duty.

There can ... be no doubt that a reasonable act performed for the purpose of self-preservation, being ... itself an act caused by the accused's own act does not operate as a *novus actus interveniens* ... if a reasonable act of self-defence against the act of the accused causes the death of a third party [there is] no reason ... why the act of self-defence, being an involuntary act caused by the act of the accused, should relieve the accused from criminal responsibility for the death of the third party.

In cases where there is an issue whether the act of the victim or the act of a third party constituted a *novus actus interveniens*, breaking the causal connection between the accused and the death of the victim, it would be appropriate for the judge to direct the jury, of course in the most simple terms, in accordance with the legal principles which they have to apply. It would then fall to the jury to decide the relevant factual issues which, identified with reference to those legal principles, will lead to the conclusion whether or not the prosecution have established the guilt of the accused of the crime of which he is charged.

Read the three extracts above and answer the questions

Questions:

1. In *White* why can the defendant not be guilty of the killing of his mother?
2. What is a 'break in the chain of causation'?
3. Why, according to Lawton LJ, is there no break in the chain of causation in *Blaue*?
4. What do you think of the defence argument that there should be no conviction because the refusal to have a blood transfusion was unreasonable?
5. What exactly is 'causation' in law?
6. Why was Pagett convicted and the police not responsible for the death of his girlfriend?

Revision exercise:
TRUE OR FALSE: on *Actus reus*

Below are 10 statements about the *actus reus*. In the column on the right, identify whether the statement is true or false.

1	*Actus reus* is criminal intent	
2	*Actus reus* requires an act	
3	*Larsonneur* is a case involving absolute liability	
4	*White* is a case used to illustrate legal causation	
5	A defendant always escapes liability when there is also medical negligence	
6	*Actus reus* must involve voluntary behaviour	
7	Liability for an omission results because there is a duty to act	
8	*Pagett* is a good illustration of legal causation	
9	Miller was not guilty	
10	A victim refusing medical treatment is a *novus actus interveniens*	

Guess the case!

Fig 1.1

With the exception of 'strict liability' offences, all crimes require criminal intent, known as '*mens rea*'. In general, three states of mind lead to criminal liability. The first is intention, which is not always easy to show and sometimes has to be inferred, so one problem is foresight of consequences. The second is recklessness. There are two types: subjective, which is appreciating the existence of an unjustified risk but still taking it; and objective, which is the taking of an obvious risk. Gross negligence applies to manslaughter and involves falling so far below the standards of a duty that is owed that it amounts to a crime and justifies more than mere compensation, as would be the civil remedy. Strict liability offences require no particular mental state but are hard to determine, usually. A further issue is the fact that the defendant's criminal intent can be transferred from the intended victim to an actual but unintended victim. This is known as 'transferred malice', though it cannot be used to transfer criminal intent between completely different crimes. A final issue is whether the *mens rea* and the *actus reus* have to be coincidental or whether, though they occur at different times, they can be said to be part of the same transaction.

2.1 Intention

Extract adapted from 'Intention and recklessness', Denis Lanser, *The Legal Executive Journal* (1995) November L.Ex

Though liability in criminal law is generally incurred by those who act either intentionally or recklessly, there are some offences for which only intention will suffice.

Examples include murder, wounding and causing grievous bodily harm with intent under the Offences Against the Person Act 1861 section 18 and attempts, at any rate, so as to any consequences in the *actus reus* of the full offence.

In seeking to understand the approach of the courts to the meaning of intention, it is advisable not to become entangled in the complications of the cases which were decided prior to *Moloney* in 1985.

... the trilogy of cases, *Moloney, Hancock and Shankland* and *Nedrick* seem to have established the current approach and to be of universal application. The key features of the approach are:

- the absence of any clear definition of intention;
- the assertion that little guidance on the meaning of intention need be given to the jury in the ordinary run of cases because the jury can be expected to recognise it when they see it;
- insistence that foresight of consequences alone is not the same thing as intention, though it can be evidence of intention (the jury can infer intention if it wishes) if it amounts to foresight of virtual certainty that the consequences will occur.
- Guidance on the latter aspect should only be given to juries in cases where it is clearly necessary.

In most cases, where the issue of intention is raised, there will be no need for the judge to complicate matters by trying to define it. This approach has considerable limitations and the disadvantages of any clear definition of intention are all too evident when the case is not a simple one. Thus a common sense approach does not yield an obvious answer to the question 'did Hancock and Shankland intend death or serious injury?', since they could claim to have been intent merely on blocking the road and disrupting the convoy.

In such cases our perception of the blameworthiness of the conduct is very much bound up with our perception of the likelihood that the consequences will occur and with our views as to the *accused's* perception of that likelihood.

In other words, if we are satisfied that the accused foresaw the consequences as virtually certain or very highly probable, we may wish to conclude that he *should* be guilty because, in terms of blameworthiness, that state of mind is indistinguishable from intention.

Nevertheless, the current approach would deny the simple equating of the one state of mind with the other. Instead, the jury is required to take a further step in any offence requiring proof of intention. That step is to *draw the inference* that the accused *intended* the consequence from proof that he foresaw it.

The jury is invited somehow to infer from one state of mind (foresight), a qualitatively different state of mind (intention) despite the fact that they have been given no guidance as to what intention means and that they may have initially decided that they were not satisfied of its existence!

In attempting to escape from the uncertainties of the approach adopted in *Hyam* where, as a matter of law, foresight of any degree of probability (as distinct from possibility) of death or serious injury would have sufficed, the courts have established a clear rule that mere foresight is not enough and promptly obscured it by opening up an alternative route through 'inference' from foresight.

If the Law Commission's proposals on intention in non-fatal offences were to be adopted and applied to all offences, these particular difficulties would certainly be reduced, if not eliminated entirely. Intention would be defined *and* that definition would include not only having the purpose of causing a consequence but also, though not having that purpose, being aware that it will occur in the ordinary course of events if the accused were to succeed in his purpose of causing some other consequence.

The Law Commission's commentary makes it plain that 'in the ordinary course of events' it covers only consequences recognised by the accused as 'near inevitable' and cites as an example an explosion designed to destroy an aeroplane in mid-air so as to claim insurance on the cargo but which will inevitably kill the crew and passengers.

If the 'virtual certainty' which *Nedrick* demands must be proved to have been foreseen before the jury is entitled (but not bound) to infer intention is co-extensive with 'aware that it would occur in the ordinary course of events', then this change would eliminate the requirement for the jury to *infer* the intention. That awareness would be intention.

Questions:

1. Which cases does Denis Lanser suggest contain the main strands of modern thinking on intention?
2. What does Denis Lanser see as the major features to come from these cases?
3. In the article, what does Denis Lanser suggest are the three main strands to the approach taken by the courts to intention?
4. How does Denis Lanser suggest that our perception of intention is tied in with our own perception of blameworthiness?
5. What were the 'uncertainties in *Hyam*' identified to in the article?
6. Why is *Hyam* a bad case?
7. What does the Law Commission's definition of 'intention' include, according to the article?
8. In what ways do you think that this would have the effect that Denis Lanser says it would have?

2.2 Recklessness

Extract adapted from the judgment in *R v Cunningham* [1957] 2 QB 396, CA

Facts

Cunningham ripped a coin-operated gas meter from the basement wall of a house in order to take the money in it. As the result of this, gas then leaked from the pipes into the next-door house, into the adjoining property. Cunningham was then convicted of maliciously administering a noxious substance, contrary to s23 Offences Against the Person Act 1861, on the trial judge's direction that the jury could convict if satisfied that his actions were 'wicked'. He appealed, successfully, on this interpretation of 'malice'.

Judgment

BYRNE J:

... the following principle was propounded by the late Professor CS Kenny in the first edition of his *Outlines of Criminal Law* ... 'In any statutory definition of a crime, malice must be taken not in the old vague sense of wickedness in general but as requiring either (1) An actual intention to do the particular kind of harm that in fact was done; or (2) recklessness as to whether such harm should occur or not (i.e. the accused has foreseen that the particular kind of harm might be done and yet has gone on to take the risk of it). It is neither limited to nor does it indeed require any ill will towards the person injured'. The same principle is repeated by Mr Turner in his 10th edition ...

We think that this is an accurate statement of the law. It derives some support from the judgments of Lord Coleridge CJ and Blackburn J in *Pembliton*'s case. In our opinion the word 'maliciously' in a statutory crime postulates foresight of the consequences.

With the utmost respect to the learned judge, we think that it is incorrect to say that the word 'malicious' in a statutory offence merely means wicked. We think the judge was, in effect, telling the jury that if they were satisfied that the appellant had acted wickedly – and he had clearly acted wickedly in stealing the gas meter and its contents – they ought to find that he had acted maliciously in causing the gas to be taken by Mrs Wade so as to thereby endanger her life.

In our view it should have been left to the jury to decide whether, even if the appellant did not intend to injure Mrs Wade, he foresaw that the removal of the gas meter might cause injury to someone but nevertheless removed it. We are unable to say that a reasonable jury, properly directed as to the meaning of the word 'maliciously' in the context of s23, would without doubt have convicted.

Extract adapted from the judgment in *Elliott v C (a Minor)* [1983] 77 Cr App R 103

Facts
A 14-year-old girl of low intelligence and in a remedial class at school stayed out all night without sleep, in a garden shed. She poured white spirit onto carpet in the shed and lit it. The shed was destroyed and she was charged under the Criminal Damage Act 1971. Magistrates acquitted her because they believed that, because of her age, lack of intelligence and lack of sleep, there would have been no obvious risk of damage. The prosecution appealed by way of case stated and the divisional court, applying Caldwell, felt compelled to allow the appeal.

Judgment

GLIDEWELL J:
Mr Moses submits that the phrase 'creates an obvious risk' means that the risk must be one which must have been obvious to a reasonably prudent man, not necessarily to the particular defendant if he or she had given thought to it.

It follows, says Mr Moses, that if the risk is one which would have been obvious to a reasonably prudent person, once it has also been proved that the particular defendant gave no thought to the possibility of there being such a risk, it is not a defence that because of limited intelligence or exhaustion she would not have appreciated the risk even if she had thought about it.

In the light of the authorities we are in my judgment bound to hold that the word 'reckless' in section 1 of the Criminal Damage Act 1971 has the meaning ascribed to it by Mr Moses.

ROBERT GOFF LJ:
I agree with the conclusion reached by Glidewell J but I do so simply because I believe myself constrained to do so by authority.

This is not a case where there was a deliberate disregard of a known risk of damage or injury of a certain type or degree; nor is it a case where there was a mindless indifference to a risk of such damage or injury; nor is it even a case where failure to give thought to the possibility of the risk was due to some blameworthy cause such as intoxication. This is a case where it appears that the only basis upon which the accused might be held to have been reckless would be if the appropriate test to be applied was purely objective – a test which in some circumstances might be thought justifiable. But such a test does not appear at first sight to be appropriate to a crime such as that under consideration in the present case.

Read the two extracts above and answer the questions

Questions:

1. What definition of the word 'maliciously' is identified in the case of *Cunningham*?
2. How is 'recklessness' defined in the same case?
3. What is the subjective element in subjective recklessness?
4. Why did the appeal succeed in *Cunningham*?
5. What different definition of recklessness is apparent from the judgment of Glidewell J in *Elliott v C*?
6. What is an 'obvious risk'?
7. Why did Robert Goff LJ agree with the conclusion in *Elliott v C* only because he felt 'constrained to do so by authority'?

 ## Gross negligence

Extract from the judgment in *R v Bateman* (1925) 19 Cr App Rep 8, CCA

Facts
The defendant was a doctor who had attended a difficult childbirth and who had negligently damaged the woman's uterus and failed to remove the woman to hospital for five days, resulting in her death. His appeal

against conviction succeeded as he was carrying out normal medical procedures, even if the procedures were faulty.

Judgment

LORD HEWART CJ:

If A has caused the death of B by alleged negligence, then, in order to establish civil liability, the plaintiff must prove ... that A owed a duty to B ... that that duty was not discharged, and that the default caused the death of B. To convict A of manslaughter, the prosecution must prove the three things above ... and that A's negligence amounted to a crime. In the civil action ... the extent of his liability depends not on the degree of negligence, but on the amount of damage done. In a criminal court, on the contrary, the amount and degree of negligence are the determining question.

In explaining to juries the test which they should apply to determine whether the negligence, in the particular case, amounted or did not amount to a crime, judges have used many epithets, such as 'culpable', 'criminal', 'gross', 'wicked', 'clear', 'complete'. But whatever epithet be used, and whether an epithet be used or not, in order to establish criminal liability the facts must be such that, in the opinion of the jury, the negligence of the accused went beyond a mere matter of compensation between subjects and showed such disregard for the life and safety of others as to amount to a crime against the state and conduct deserving punishment.

Extract adapted from 'Is the supplier also the killer?', Laurence Toczek, *New Law Journal*, 19 April 2002

In *Dias* [where the defendant had supplied a syringe of heroin to the victim who used it immediately and later died from an overdose] the ... trial judge directed the jury in accordance with *Kennedy* that the self-injection of heroin was an unlawful act and the defendant was convicted of manslaughter. The Court of Appeal refused to follow *Kennedy* in this respect and quashed the conviction [but] left open the possibility of manslaughter convictions in the future on the basis of an unlawful act under s23 [OAPA 1861 – unlawfully administering poison].

The Court of Appeal in *Dias* also contemplated a manslaughter conviction on the basis of gross negligence where a duty could be established. It is clear from ... *Adomako* that the defendant must have been in a breach of a duty of care under the usual principles of negligence; there must have been a risk of death; the negligence must have caused death; and the conduct of the defendant must, in the opinion of the jury, have been so bad as to amount to a criminal act or omission.

In *R v Khan and Khan* the defendants supplied a 15-year-old prostitute with heroin; she snorted some of it through her nose and ate the rest. She went into a coma but, rather than summoning medical assistance, the defendants simply left her alone. When they returned next day she was dead. They were convicted of manslaughter. The Court of Appeal, although allowing the appeals due to misdirection ..., did express the opinion that defendants of this sort might be under a duty to summon medical assistance and therefore be guilty of manslaughter. *Dias* [implies] that the duty might arise at an earlier stage, i.e. the duty not to supply the drugs in the first place.

Where a drug user dies ... police ... should ... charge [suppliers] with manslaughter ... provided they have evidence that they not only supplied the drug but also prepared it for use. In those circumstances they should consider charging them on the basis of an unlawful act under s23 of the Offences Against the Person Act 1861 or on the basis of gross negligence manslaughter.

Read the two extracts above and answer the questions

Questions:

1. What are the major elements of gross negligence manslaughter as identified by Lord Hewart in *Bateman*?
2. How does Lord Hewart CJ describe the difference between the civil standard of negligence and the criminal standard of negligence?
3. Who determines whether the defendant's acts or omissions amount to gross negligence?
4. Why did the Court of Appeal refuse to follow *Kennedy* in *Dias*?

2.4 Strict liability offences

Extract adapted from the judgment in *R v Lemon; R v Gay News Ltd* [1979] 1 All ER 898, HL

The facts appear in the judgment of Lord Diplock

Judgment

LORD DIPLOCK (dissenting):

[T]he appellants are the editor and publishers of a newspaper called Gay News. In an issue ... published in June 1976 there appeared a poem ... accompanied by a drawing illustrating its subject-matter. The poem purports to describe in detail acts of sodomy and fellatio with the body of Christ immediately after His death and to ascribe to Him during His lifetime promiscuous homosexual practices ...

The issue in this appeal is not whether the words and drawings are blasphemous. The jury ... have found them to be so ... The only question ... is whether in 1976 the mental element or *mens rea* in the common law offence of blasphemy is satisfied by proof only of an intention to publish material which in the opinion of the jury is likely to shock and arouse resentment among believing Christians or whether the prosecution must [also] prove that the accused in publishing the material in fact intended to produce that effect ... [if the former] blasphemous libel would revert to the exceptional category of crimes of strict liability ...

The usual justification for creating by statute a criminal offence of strict liability, in which the prosecution need not prove *mens rea* to one of the elements of the *actus reus*, is the threat ... to public health, public safety, public morals or public order. The very fact that there have been no prosecutions for ... more than fifty years is sufficient to dispose of any suggestion ... to include [the] offence ... in ... strict liability ...

VISCOUNT DILHORNE:
If it be accepted, as I think it must, that that which it is sought to prevent is the publication of blasphemous libels, the harm is done by their intentional publication, whether or not the publisher intended to blaspheme. To hold that it must be proved that he had that intent appears to me to be going some way to making the accused the judge in his own cause.

Guilt of the offence of publishing a blasphemous libel does not depend on the accused having an intent to blaspheme, but on proof that the publication was intentional and that the matter published was blasphemous.

Appeals dismissed.

Extract adapted from 'Mistake and strict liability – Part 1', John Beaumont, *New Law Journal*, 17 March 2000

I[n] *B v DPP* [[200] 1 All ER 833] ...The defendant was charged with inciting a girl aged under fourteen to commit an act of gross indecency with him contrary to s1(1) of the Indecency with Children Act 1960.

The facts were ... A girl aged 13 was a passenger on a bus. The defendant, who was 15, sat next to her. He asked her to perform oral sex with him. She refused. He repeated his request several times and she repeatedly refused. It was accepted that [he] honestly believed that the girl was over 14.

At the trial the magistrates were asked to rule as to whether his state of mind constituted a defence ... they ruled it did not ... The Divisional Court upheld the magistrates' decision and the defendant appealed to the House of Lords.

Section 1(1) of the ... Act is a typical provision of its time in that [it] says nothing about the mental element. ...Lord Nicholls pointed out ... [that this means] that the court must start out from the established common law presumption that *mens rea* was an essential ingredient unless Parliament had indicated a contrary intention. In the key case on strict liability, *Sweet v Parsley [1969] 1 All ER 347* ... passages from the judgment of Lord Reid ... illustrate this:

'[W]henever a section is silent as to *mens rea* there is a presumption that, in order to give effect to the will of Parliament, we must read in words appropriate to *mens rea*.'

'[I]t is a universal principle that if a penal provision is reasonably capable of two interpretations, that the interpretation which is most favourable to the defendant must be adopted.'

In *B v DPP* Lord Nicholls ... endorsed the principles to be found in *Sweet v Parsley*.

[On] the principles to be applied in a case where the statute in question does not expressly mention *mens rea*, Lord Nicholls examined the factors to be examined in considering whether Parliament's intention was to impose strict liability by 'necessary implication' .. . any necessary implication could only be satisfied [if] 'compellingly clear'. His Lordship gave ... examples ...

'It might be found in the language used, the nature of the offence, the mischief sought to be prevented and any other circumstances that might assist in determining what intention was properly to be attributed to Parliament.'

According to his Lordship ... the position here was relatively straightforward ... what was, when enacted, an entirely new offence ... set out in simple and straightforward language [and] a serious offence.

'The more serious the offence, the greater was the weight to be attached to the presumption, because the more grave was the punishment and the graver the stigma that accompanied a conviction.'

Lord Nicholls stated that the fact that the conduct might range from what was depraved by any acceptable standard to what was relatively innocuous behaviour in private between two young people reinforced, rather than negatived, the application of the presumption.

Another factor ... is ... that the purpose of s1(1) of the 1960 Act was to protect children. The House was ... of the opinion that that factor did not lead ... to the conclusion that liability had intended to be strict so far as ... age ... was concerned.

A final factor is whether strict liability would further the purpose of section 1(1) more effectively than if *mens rea* were read into the offence. Lord Nicholls [pointed] out that there was no general agreement that strict liability was necessary to the enforcement of the law protecting children in sexual matters. Some commentators argue ... if the whole point of the section is to protect young girls, then this will be undermined if a person can put forward a defence ... that the girl looked older. However, if ... *mens rea* involves ... recklessness ... this solve[s] any problem.

Accordingly, the House could not find ... sufficient cogency to displace the application of the common law principle of *mens rea*.

However, the case does not really make any progress to solve the general problem of when strict liability should be imposed.

... Lord Hutton said that it is to be regretted that Parliament has not taken account of expert advice ... from law reform bodies ... that Parliament should address its mind in enacting legislation ... to the issue of whether *mens rea* should be a constituent part of the offences and should state in clear terms whether or not *mens rea* is required.

Read the two extracts above and answer the questions

Questions:

1. What exactly is a crime of strict liability?
2. On what basis did their Lordships determine that there was a crime of strict liability in *R v Lemon*?
3. On what basis could the House of Lords not find that there was a crime of strict liability in *B v DPP*?

2.5 Transferred malice

Extract from *Attorney-General's Reference (No 3 of 1994)* [1997] 3 WLR 421, HL

Facts

The respondent had stabbed his pregnant girlfriend in the stomach. Doctors failed to spot the injuries to the foetus and when it was born prematurely it died later, not from the stab wounds but from the premature birth and from complications associated with it. The reference to the Court of Appeal was on two questions: whether deliberate infliction of injury to an unborn child or its mother can be murder or manslaughter where the child is born alive but later dies wholly or partly from the injuries inflicted on it while in the womb; and whether the fact that the death results solely as a result of the injuries to the mother negatives the murder or manslaughter of the child. Both issues were referred to the House of Lords.

Judgment

LORD MUSTILL:
I find it hard to base a modern law of murder on these two cases [*Latimer* and *Pembliton*]. The court in *Latimer* was, I believe, entirely justified in finding a distinction between their statutory backgrounds and one can well accept that the answers given, one for acquittal, the other for conviction, would be the same today. But the harking back to a concept of general malice, which amounts to no more than this, that a wrongful act displays malevolence which can be attached to any adverse consequence, has long been out of date. And to speak of a particular malice which is 'transferred' simply disguises the problem by idiomatic language. The defendant's malice is directed at one objective, and when after the event the court treats it as directed at another object it is not recognising a 'transfer' but creating a new malice which never existed before.

... the purpose of this enquiry has been to see whether the existing rules are based on principles sound enough to justify their extension to a case where the defendant acts without an intent to injure either the foetus or the child which it will become. In my opinion they are not.

The effect of transferred malice, as I understand it, is that the intended victim and the actual victim are treated as if they were one, so that what was intended to happen to the first person (but did not happen) is added to what actually did happen to the second person (but was not intended to happen), with the result that what was intended and what happened are married to make a notionally intended and actually constituted crime. The cases are treated as if the actual victim had been the intended victim from the start. To make any sense of this process there must ... be some compatibility between the original intention and the actual occurrence ... There is no such compatibility here.

Questions:

1. What exactly is transferred malice?
2. What is the difference between the cases of *Latimer* and *Pembliton*?
3. What does Lord Mustill consider to be the problem with the traditional law?
4. How was malice 'transferred' in the case here?

2.6 Coincidence of the *actus reus* and the *mens rea*

Extract from *Thabo Meli v R* [1954] 1 All ER 373

Facts

The appellants took a man to a hut, gave him beer and then struck him over the head to kill him. Believing him to be dead, they rolled his body over a cliff and made it look like an accident. In fact the man was not dead but died later from exposure. They failed in their appeal from conviction.

Judgment

LORD REID:
The point of law ... can be simply stated. It is said that two acts were done: – first, the attack in the hut; secondly, the placing of the body outside afterwards – and that they were separate acts. It is said that while the first act was accompanied by *mens rea*, it was not the cause of death; but that the second act, while it was the cause of death, was not accompanied by *mens rea*; and on that ground, it is said that the accused are not guilty of murder ... there could be no intention to kill when the accused thought that the man was already dead, so their original intention to kill had ceased before they did the act that caused the man's death. It appears ... impossible to divide up what was really one series of acts in this way. Their crime is not reduced from murder to a lesser crime merely because the accused were under some misapprehension for a time during the completion of their criminal plot.

Extract from *Fagan v Metropolitan Police Commissioner* [1969] 1 QB 439

Facts

A police officer directed the appellant to stop in a particular spot. In doing so he accidentally drove on to the constable's foot. He then failed to reverse the car when requested and left it there for some time. He unsuccessfully appealed against conviction.

Judgment

JAMES J:
... the crucial question is whether ... the act of the appellant can be said to be complete ... at the moment of time when the car wheel came to rest on the foot, or whether his act is to be regarded as a continuing act operating until the wheel was removed ... a distinction is to be drawn between acts which are complete – though results may continue to flow – and those acts which are continuing ... It is not necessary that *mens rea* should be present at the inception of the *actus reus*, it can be superimposed on an existing act. On the other hand, the subsequent inception of *mens rea* cannot convert an act which has been completed without *mens rea* into an assault.

There was an act constituting a battery which at its inception was not criminal because there was no element of intention, but which became criminal from the moment the intention was formed to produce the apprehension which was flowing from the continuing act.

Read the two extracts above and answer the questions

Questions:

1. What is in effect the argument of the appellant in either case?
2. What, if anything, distinguishes the two cases?
3. Is there any real difference in the reasoning for dismissing both appeals?

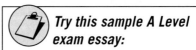 **Try this sample A Level exam essay:**

Critically discuss the way in which the courts have attempted to define 'intention'.

Revision exercise:
MENS REA CROSSWORD

Answer the clues 1–8 in the spaces in the crossword below to find out what the shaded box, reading across, says about the defendant's state of mind.

CLUES
1. More than careless, I should say
2. Sounds rather large for a mental state and may be disgusting in another context
3. Like some schoolteachers, this liability is!
4. No transfer to a different offence in this case
5. Sounds more like tort than crime, but could join up with 2
6. A case to associate with 1, subjectively speaking
7. Sounds really spiteful, despite its significance to murder
8. My computer-literate friends call it forward slash – but it's not a direct way of showing intent

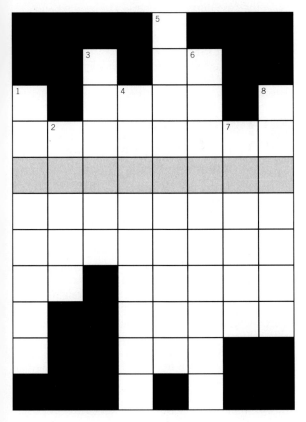

Guess the case!

Fig 2.1

CHAPTER 3

UNLAWFUL KILLING: MURDER

Murder is the most serious crime. It involves an unlawful killing of a living human being by a sane defendant of the appropriate age, ie over ten years old, who intends to kill or to cause grievous bodily harm to the victim. Problems associated with the *actus reus* of murder can involve causation and the status of the victim. Problems to do with the *mens rea* usually involve proving the necessary intention in which the relevance of foresight of consequences is always a prominent and difficult factor.

 Actus reus

Extract adapted from 'Criminal Law Text and Materials', CMV Clarkson and HM Keating, Sweet & Maxwell, 1998, p 632

The elements of the *actus reus*:

1. *'unlawfully'*: some killings, such as those in self-defence, may be justified and therefore lawful.

2. *'killing'*: the act (or omission) of the defendant must have killed the victim; it must have been the legal cause of the death of the victim. Causation must be established.

3. *'a reasonable person who is in being'*: the victim must be a human being who was alive at the time of the defendant's actions. This raises problems ... as to the precise moment when life begins and ends. In view of developments with heart transplant operations and life support machines the problem of determining the exact moment of death has assumed some importance in recent years ... a foetus is not a human being for the purposes of the law of homicide.

4. *'under the King's Peace'*: all human beings are under the 'Queen's peace' except an alien enemy 'in the heat of war'.

Questions:

1. The *actus reus* of an offence can include conduct, circumstances and consequences. In the case of murder, what is the conduct and what are the consequences?
2. What problems can arise in relation to the victim of the offence?
3. What exactly does 'residing under the Queen's Peace' mean?

 Mens rea

Extract adapted from 'Summing up intention', Simon Cooper, *New Law Journal*, 18 August 2000

The concept of intention in criminal law has long troubled many talented lawyers. There cannot be too many examples of a legal concept having such a turbulent time both at the hands of the academics and the judges. Yet, ask a layman what 'intention' means and you are certain to receive the same straightforward answer. The layman will tell you that intention (to kill, for example) means 'to want to kill' or 'to mean to kill' or 'to desire to kill'. There is no dispute that a defendant who *desires* to achieve a particular consequence or *means* to achieve it, intends it. Beyond that, there is difficulty.

The overwhelming majority of difficult cases have been concerned with the meaning of intention when the defendant is alleged to have committed murder *and* it is suggested that the desire or aim of the defendant was something other than to kill. ... the law has concluded that a jury is entitled to find a defendant intended a consequence if it was virtually certain to occur.

Here, I am concerned about ... the criminal liability of doctors who administer pain relieving drugs that also have the effect of ending the life of the recipient notwithstanding that recipient is terminally ill and perhaps already close to death.

In order to convict a defendant of murder, it is the duty of the prosecution to prove beyond a reasonable doubt that the defendant (i) caused the death ... (ii) did so with intent to kill or to cause grievous bodily harm. ... In *Adams* a doctor administered ... morphine to a terminally ill patient who died as a consequence of the drug ... Devlin J focused on causation and said: '[in what] circumstances [might] doctors ... be justified in administering drugs which would shorten life. Cases of severe pain have been suggested ... the law knows of no special defence of this character.'

In *Cox* Ognall J said 'There can be no doubt that the use of drugs to relieve pain and suffering will often be fully justified notwithstanding that it will ... hasten the moment of death. What can never be lawful is the use of death with the primary purpose of hastening the moment of death.'

In *Moor*, Hooper J directed the jury by means of ... questions, two of which ... concerned ... intention.

1. ... are you sure that Dr Moor's purpose in giving the ... injection was not to give treatment which he believed in the circumstances to be proper treatment to relieve ... pain and suffering? If ... 'No' your verdict must be 'Not guilty'. If ... 'Yes' ...
2. are you sure that the defendant when he gave the ... injection intended to kill ...? If ... no, your verdict must be 'Not guilty'.

The issue, which must be of prime concern, is whether or not doctors have now been provided with some kind of special defence to a charge of murder ... JC Smith concludes that the judge's question 1, above must [do so] notwithstanding the courts' insistence that the law is the same for doctors as for everyone else. The question clearly suggests that a doctor who has caused death is not guilty of murder if the purpose of the treatment was to relieve pain and suffering and was 'proper treatment'.

It cannot be right that the concept of intention appears to spawn a 'special defence' based solely upon the identity of the person accused ... It is unsatisfactory for doctors, patients and relatives, not to mention lawyers.

Extract adapted from the judgment in *R v Moloney, Times Law Report*, 22 March 1985

Facts

A stepfather and stepson who were both rather drunk were playing with a loaded shotgun. Moloney claimed that they argued as to who could load and shoot the gun quickest, that the stepfather encouraged him to fire and that he just fired the gun without aiming and the next thing he knew was that his stepfather was dead. Moloney was convicted but the House of Lords eventually accepted his appeal.

Judgment

LORD BRIDGE:
The golden rule should be that, when directing a jury on the mental element necessary in a crime of specific intent, the judge should avoid any elaboration or paraphrase of what is meant by intent and leave it to the jury's good sense to decide whether the accused acted with the necessary intent ...

Starting from the proposition that the mental element in murder requires proof of an intention to kill or cause really serious injury, the first fundamental question to be answered is whether there is any rule of substantive law that foresight by the accused of one of those eventualities as a probable consequence of his voluntary act was equivalent or alternative to the necessary intention. I would answer this question in the negative.

Foresight of consequences, as an element bearing on the issue of intention in murder, or indeed any other crime of specific intent, belongs, not to the substantive law, but to the law of evidence.

In the rare cases in which it was necessary to direct a jury by reference to foresight of consequences, I do not believe that it is necessary for the judge to do more than invite the jury to consider two questions:

First, was death or really serious injury in a murder case a natural consequence of the defendant's voluntary act? Second, did the defendant foresee that consequence as being a natural consequence of his act? ... if they answered yes to both questions it was a proper inference for them to draw that he intended the consequence.

Extract adapted from the judgment in *R v Hancock and Shankland* [1986] AC 455, HL

Facts

Two striking miners during the miners' strike of 1984 pushed a heavy concrete block and a concrete post off a bridge into the path of a taxi taking another miner to work, in order to frighten the other miner. In fact, the block went through the windscreen, killing the taxi driver. The miners denied that they had intended any harm, claiming that they had only intended to block the road. The Crown refused to accept a plea of guilty to manslaughter and the miners were convicted of murder. In the House of Lords the court had to consider whether there was sufficient *mens rea* for murder.

Judgment

LORD SCARMAN:

First the House cleared away the confusions which had obscured the law during the last 25 years laying down authoritatively that the mental element of murder is a specific intent, the intent to kill or to inflict serious bodily harm. Nothing less suffices: and the jury must be sure that the intent existed when the act was done which resulted in death before they can return a verdict of murder.

Secondly the House made it absolutely clear that foresight of consequences is no more than evidence of the existence of the intent; it must be considered, and its weight assessed, together with all the evidence in the case. Foresight does not necessarily imply the existence of intention, though it may be a fact from which when considered with all the other evidence a jury may think it right to infer the necessary intent.

Thirdly, the House emphasised that the probability of the result of an act is an important matter for the jury to consider and can be critical in their determining whether the result was intended.

Read the three extracts above and answer the questions

Questions:

1. How is the necessary mental element for murder defined in the sources?
2. How does Simon Cooper's article define the intent to kill?
3. What exactly is the 'special defence' that Simon Cooper is worried about?
4. Why does Lord Bridge in *Moloney* think that it will be only on rare occasions that a jury must be directed on the meaning of intention in murder?
5. In *Moloney* how does Lord Bridge describe the significance of 'foresight of consequences'?
6. According to Lord Bridge in *Moloney*, if the judge has to direct the jury, how should this be done?
7. How does Lord Scarman describe the nature of foresight in *Hancock and Shankland*?

Extract adapted from 'Foresight and foreseeability', Sean Enright, *New Law Journal*, 6 November 1998, pp 1636–1637

'Foresight and foreseeability are not the same thing as intention although either may give rise to an irresistible inference of such...' (*R v Hyam* [1985]). Difficult legal concepts neatly expressed. The wonder is that the common law is still grappling with the relationship between foresight and intention and the directions to be given to a jury in such circumstances. The latest attempt to resolve the issue in *Woollin* [1998] is likely to create as many problems as it solves.

The issue surfaced as long ago as *DPP v Smith* [1961] ... the defendant killed a policeman by driving from the scene while the officer was hanging onto the car. The Lords ruled that the defendant was guilty of murder because death was foreseen by him as a likely result of his act and that he was deemed to have foreseen the risk a reasonable person in his position would have foreseen.

The notion that *mens rea* could be imputed to a defendant facing a murder charge was bound to be unpopular. With hindsight the test was always likely to prove unworkable.

In fact *DPP v Smith* was soon overruled by Parliament implementing s8 of the Criminal Justice Act 1967 which provides:

'A court or jury in determining whether a person has committed an offence, shall not be bound by law to infer that he intended or foresaw a result of his actions by reason only of its being a natural and probable consequence of those actions; but shall decide whether he did intend or foresee that result by reference to all the evidence, drawing such inferences from the evidence as appear proper in the circumstances.'

The intervention by Parliament failed to resolve matters. In the great majority of cases there was no difficulty. Juries were directed that before convicting it was necessary to be sure that the defendant intended to kill or cause serious harm. The continuing difficulty related to that class of case where such a simple direction did not fit he facts of the case – where, for instance, a defendant's intent was not readily apparent. In these circumstances what state of mind could amount to the necessary intent to prove murder?

The next opportunity for the Lords to resolve the difficulty arose in *Hyam* [1975] which split the Lords three/two. Almost uniquely, the speeches of the three Law Lords who prevailed gave different tests to be applied on the question of intent.

Their Lordships had another bite of the cherry in *Moloney* [1985]. The House of Lords proceeded to issue guidelines on what constituted the necessary mental intent in murder. These can be summarised as follows:

- [In] a crime of specific intent ... the probability of consequences taken to have been foreseen must be little short of overwhelming before it will suffice to establish the necessary intent.
- In directing the jury, the judge should avoid any elaboration or paraphrase of what is meant by intent, and leave it to the jury's good sense to decide whether the accused acted with the necessary intent, unless the judge is convinced that, on the facts and having regard to the way the case has been presented to the jury in evidence and argument some further explanation or elaboration is strictly necessary to avoid misunderstanding.
- Foresight of consequences, as an element of bearing on the issue of intention in murder or any other crime of specific intent, belongs not to the substantive law but to the law of evidence. In the rare cases in which it is necessary for the judge to direct a jury by reference to foresight of consequences he should direct the jury to answer two questions: first, was the death or really serious injury a natural consequence of the defendant's voluntary act? Secondly, did the defendant foresee that consequence as being a natural consequence of that act? If the jury answer yes to both questions it is a proper inference to infer that he intended that consequence.

Did this settle the law? Sadly not. Further trips were made to the Lords in *Hancock and Shankland* [1986] a case in which striking miners had dropped a concrete block off a bridge. [In] the Lords it was held that where it was necessary to direct the jury on the issue of intent by reference to foresight of consequences, the judges should refer to probability and explain to the jury that the greater the probability of the consequence the more likely that it was foreseen, and that if it was foreseen the more likely it was that it was intended.

If anyone thought that this would unscramble the mess they were sadly mistaken. *Nedrick* [1986] was another arson case which raised the same old difficulties of proving intent from actions. The Court of Appeal created complications by adding words of advice to trial judges: '... the jury should be directed that a person may intend a certain result while not desiring it to come about; in determining whether the defendant had the necessary intent, they may find it helpful to ask themselves, first how probable was the consequence that resulted from his voluntary act and, secondly, whether he foresaw that consequence; he could not have intended to bring death or serious harm about if he did not appreciate that death or serious harm was likely to result from his act. If he thought that the risk to which he was exposing the deceased was only slight the jury may easily conclude that he did not intend to bring about the death; the jury should be directed that they are not entitled to infer the necessary intention unless they feel sure that death or serious harm was a virtual certainty and that he appreciated that was the case'.

Nedrick at last brings us to *Woollin* [who] lost his temper and threw his three-month old son onto a hard surface. The son sustained a fractured skull and died. At the trial, the prosecution did not contend that the appellant had desired to kill his son or to cause him serious injury. The issue was whether the appellant had the intent to cause serious harm.

Subject to one qualification the trial judge had summed up in accordance with guidance given by Lane CJ in *Nedrick* and gave the jury what has become known as the 'virtual certainty' direction. ... the judge diluted the test by directing the jury that it was open to them to convict if they found that the appellant must have realised and appreciated when he threw the child that there was a substantial risk that he would cause the child serious injury. The jury convicted of murder.

Following an unsuccessful appearance before the Court of Appeal the following questions of public importance were certified:

'In murder, where there is no direct evidence that the purpose of the defendant was to kill or inflict serious harm on the victim, is it necessary to direct a jury that they may only infer an intent to do serious injury if they are satisfied

- That serious bodily harm was a virtually certain consequence of the defendant's voluntary act and

- That the defendant appreciated that fact? If the answer to question 1 is "yes" is such a direction necessary in all cases or is it only necessary in cases where the sole evidence of the defendant's intention is to be found in his actions and their consequences to the victim?'

Their Lordships declined to answer the certified question ... It is plain that their Lordships found that the direction by the trial judge diluted the *Nedrick* direction to such an extent that the distinction between recklessness and murder was blurred.

On the wider issue as to whether *Nedrick* was correctly decided, the Lords approved the *Nedrick* test on virtual certainty describing it as 'a tried and tested formula. Trial judges ought to continue to use it'. It is important to note that the *Nedrick* test continues to apply to that class of murder case where exceptionally, the usual direction on intention to kill or cause serious harm is though to be insufficient.

Lord Steyn and Lord Hope observed that the two subsidiary questions posed by the Court of Appeal in *Nedrick*: 'how probable was the consequence? Did he foresee that consequence?' ought never be put to a jury.

Woollin raised some important difficulties. At the heart of the debate lies the notion of 'intent', a concept quite different from motive, desire or foresight ... academics and judges tend to fight shy of definitions of intent. Instead, the debate has focused on the means by which intent can be proved or inferred.

The direction in *Woollin* comes perilously close to implementing the imputed knowledge test in *DPP v Smith*. Equally a direction given pursuant to *Woollin* would appear to prevent the jury construing intent in accordance with s8 of the Criminal Justice Act 1967.

There are other difficulties: a person may be convicted as an accessory, on the basis that he hoped that the principal would not use violence but realising that lethal violence might be used. The principal offender to the same murder might escape liability if the jury found that he foresaw the consequences of his action would probably lead to death.

Extract adapted from the judgment in *R v Woollin* [1998] 3 WLR 382

Facts

A father, in a fit of temper, threw his three-month-old son onto a hard floor. The boy died from a fractured skull. The father's plea of provocation failed and he was convicted of manslaughter. This conviction was overturned and a verdict of manslaughter substituted by the House of Lords.

Judgment

LORD STEYN:

In *Hancock* Lord Scarman did not express disagreement with the test of foresight of a probability which is 'little short of overwhelming' as enunciated in *Moloney*. Lord Scarman also did not express disagreement with the law underlying Lord Lane's model direction in *Hancock* which was based on a defendant having 'appreciated that what he did was highly likely to cause death or really serious bodily injury.' Lord Scarman merely said that model directions were generally undesirable. Moreover, Lord Scarman thought that where explanation is required the jury should be directed as to the relevance of probability without expressly stating the matter in terms of any particular level of probability. The manner in which trial judges were to direct juries was left unclear. Moreover, in practice juries sometimes ask probing questions which cannot easily be ignored by trial judges. For example, imagine that in a case such as *Hancock* the jury sent a note to the judge to the following effect:

> 'We are satisfied that the defendant, though he did not want to cause serious harm, knew that it was probable that his act would cause serious bodily harm. We are not sure whether a probability is enough for murder. Please explain.'

One may alter the question by substituting 'highly probable' for 'probable'. Or one may imagine the jury asking whether a foresight of a 'substantial risk' that the defendant's act would cause serious injury was enough. What is the judge to say to the jury? *Hancock* does not rule out an answer by the judge but it certainly does not explain how such questions are to be answered. It is well known that judges were sometimes advised to deflect such questions by the statement that 'intention' is an ordinary word in the English language. That is surely an unhelpful response to what may be a sensible question. In these circumstances it is not altogether surprising that in *Nedrick* the Court of Appeal felt compelled to provide a model direction for the assistance of trial judges.

Read the two extracts above and answer the questions

Questions:

1. In Sean Enright's article, what problem does he identify in the case of *DPP v Smith*?
2. How far do you think s8 of the Criminal Justice Act 1967 overcame that problem?
3. Following *Moloney*, when, according to the article, will a judge need to direct a jury on the issue of intention?
4. How, according to the article, does the judgment in *Hancock and Shankland* elaborate on the issue of foresight of consequences?
5. What extra point was added by *Nedrick*?
6. In *Woollin*, why do you think Sean Enright suggests that 'their Lordships found that the direction by the trial judge diluted the *Nedrick* direction to such an extent that the distinction between recklessness and murder was blurred'?
7. In the extract from *Woollin*, how does Lord Steyn justify the 'model direction' in *Nedrick*?
8. In what ways is Sean Enright's comment that the judgment in *Woollin* 'comes perilously close to implementing the imputed knowledge test in *DPP v Smith*' accurate?

4. .... can be both direct or .... In the first it can be shown that the defendant .... the consequences. In the latter it is for the jury to .... the intent from the circumstances of the case.
5. The model direction from .... Is that if it is necessary for a judge to direct a .... on .... of consequences they should be asked to answer two questions: first, was .... or really .... a natural consequence of the defendant's voluntary act? If so, did the defendant .... that consequence as being a natural consequence of that act?

 ### Try this sample A Level exam essay:

Discuss the extent to which *mens rea* in murder has now become settled through many judicial decisions which make it unnecessary for Parliament to legislate.

Revision exercises:
MISSING LINKS

In each of the following short statements, fill in the missing words to complete the passages accurately.

1. In murder, the person carrying out the crime must be both ...... and a person over the age of ....
2. The *actus reus* of murder involves an .... killing of another living .... residing under the .... There is no longer any requirement that the death should occur within .. ..
3. The *mens rea* for murder is .... This is where the defendant .... to kill or .... to cause serious ....

CHAPTER 4

UNLAWFUL KILLING: VOLUNTARY MANSLAUGHTER

Voluntary manslaughter occurs where the defendant has both the *actus reus* and the necessary *mens rea* for murder. The defendant pleads one of three partial defences identified in the Homicide Act 1957 which, if successful, have the effect of reducing the charge to manslaughter and removing the mandatory life sentence. Diminished responsibility involves an 'abnormality of the mind'. Provocation involves conduct by the victim which has caused the defendant to lose self-control and reasonable people would have similarly reacted. Failed suicide pacts obviously mean that one party has survived. Interesting features of provocation are the characteristics of the defendant that can be taken into account, and the difficulties faced by battered women who try to use the plea.

 4.1

Diminished responsibility

Extract from the Homicide Act 1957 (s2)

2. Persons suffering from diminished responsibility

(1) Where a person kills or is party to the killing of another, he shall not be convicted of murder if he was suffering from such abnormality of mind (whether arising from a condition of arrested or retarded development of mind or any inherent causes or induced by disease or injury) as substantially impaired his mental responsibility for his acts and omissions in doing or being a party to the killing.

(3) A person who but for this section would be liable, whether as principal or as accessory, to be convicted of murder shall be liable instead to be convicted of manslaughter.

Extract adapted from the judgment in *R v Byrne* [1960] 2 QB 396

Facts

Byrne was convicted of the murder of a young girl who he had strangled and whose body he had afterwards horribly mutilated. His defence was that he was suffering from diminished responsibility. Evidence given by specialist psychologists at the trial showed that he was a 'sexual psychopath' driven by uncontrollable and perverted sexual desires. His appeal was allowed and a verdict of manslaughter substituted, although his life sentence was not altered.

Judgment

LORD PARKER CJ
'Abnormality of mind,' which has to be contrasted with

the time-honoured expression in the M'Naghten Rules 'defect of reason,' means a state of mind so different from that of ordinary human beings that the reasonable man would term it abnormal. It appears to us to be wide enough to cover the mind's activities in all its aspects, not only the perception of physical acts and matters, and the ability to form a rational judgment as to whether an act is right or wrong, but also the ability to exercise will power to control physical acts in accordance with that rational judgment. The expression 'mental responsibility for his acts' points to a consideration of the extent to which the accused's mind is answerable for his physical acts which must include a consideration of the extent of his ability to exercise will power to control his physical acts.

Whether the accused was at the time of the killing suffering from any 'abnormality of the mind' in the broad sense which we have indicated is a question for the jury. On this question medical evidence is no doubt important, but the jury are entitled to take into consideration all the evidence, including the acts or statements of the accused and his demeanour.

Assuming that the jury are satisfied that the accused was suffering from 'abnormality of mind' from one of the causes specified in the parenthesis '[inside the brackets]' of the subsection, the crucial question nevertheless arises: was the abnormality such as substantially impaired his mental responsibility for his acts in doing or being a party to the killing? This is a question of degree and essentially one for the jury.

Furthermore, in a case where the abnormality of mind is one which affects the accused's self-control the step between 'he did not resist his impulse' and 'he could not resist his impulse' is, as the evidence in this case shows, one which is incapable of scientific proof.

inability to exercise will power to control physical acts, provided that is due to abnormality of mind from one of the causes specified in the parenthesis [brackets] in the subsection is, in our view, sufficient to entitle the accused to the benefit of the section; difficulty in controlling his physical acts, depending on the degree of difficulty, may be. It is for the jury to decide on the whole of the evidence whether such inability or difficulty has, not as a matter of scientific certainty but on the balance of probabilities, been established, and in the case of difficulty whether the difficulty is so great as to amount in their view to a substantial impairment of the accused's mental responsibility for his acts.

Read the two extracts above and answer the questions

Questions:

1. What, according to s2 of the Act, will be the consequences of a successful plea of diminished responsibility?
2. How does Lord Parker explain the expression 'abnormality of mind' from s2 of the Act, and do you think that this fully explains it?
3. What part does Lord Parker think medical evidence should play in determining whether or not a plea of diminished responsibility succeeds?
4. What are the causes of the abnormality of mind 'specified in the parenthesis of the subsection' and what do they refer to?
5. In what way was Byrne suffering from diminished responsibility?

4.2 Provocation

Extract from the Homicide Act 1957 (s3)

3. Provocation

Where on a charge of murder there is evidence on which the jury can find that the person charged was provoked (whether by things done or by things said or by both together) to lose his self-control, the question whether the provocation was enough to make a reasonable man do as he did shall be left to be determined by the jury; and in determining that question the jury shall take into account everything both done and said according to the effect which in their opinion, it would have on a reasonable man.

Extract adapted from the judgment in *R v Camplin* [1978] AC 705, HL

Facts

Camplin, who was aged 15 at the time, was buggered and then mocked about the incident by an old man with whom he was alone in the old man's flat. Camplin killed the old man by splitting his skull with a large frying pan. He was convicted of murder but on appeal a verdict of manslaughter by reason of provocation was substituted.

Judgment

LORD DIPLOCK:
The point of general public importance involved in the case has been certified as being:

'Whether on the prosecution for murder of a boy of 15, where the issue of provocation arises, the jury should be directed to consider the question under section 3 of the Homicide Act 1957 whether the provocation was enough to make a reasonable man do as he did by reference to a "reasonable adult" or by reference to a "reasonable boy of 15".'

The public policy that underlay the adoption of the 'reasonable man' test in the common law doctrine of provocation was to reduce the incidence of fatal violence by preventing a person relying upon his own exceptional pugnacity or excitability as an excuse for loss of self-control. The rationale of the test may not be easy to reconcile in logic with more universal propositions as to the mental element in crime. Nevertheless it has been preserved by the Act of 1957 but falls to be applied now in the context of a law of provocation that is significantly different from what it was before the Act was passed.

Although it is now for the jury to apply the 'reasonable man' test, it still remains for the judge to direct them what, in the new context of the section, is the meaning of this apparently inapt expression ...

As I have already pointed out, for the purposes of the law of provocation the 'reasonable man' has never been confined to the adult male. It means an ordinary person of either sex, not exceptionally excitable or pugnacious, but possessed of such powers of self-control as everyone is entitled to expect that his fellow citizens will exercise in society as it is today.

... now that the law has been changed so as to permit of words being treated as provocation, even though unaccompanied by any other acts, the gravity of verbal provocation may well depend upon the particular characteristics or circumstances to whom a taunt or insult is addressed. It would stultify much of the mitigation of the previous harshness of the common law in ruling out verbal provocation as capable of reducing murder to manslaughter if the jury could not take into consideration all those factors which in their opinion would affect the gravity of taunts or insults when applied to the person to whom they are addressed. So to this extent at any rate the unqualified proposition accepted by this House in *Bedder v DPP* [1954] that for the purposes of the 'reasonable man' test any unusual physical characteristics of the accused must be ignored requires revision as a result of the passing of the Act of 1957.

That he was only 15 years of age at the time of the killing is the relevant characteristic of the accused in the instant case. It is a characteristic which may have its effects on temperament as well as physique. If the jury think that the same power of self-control is not to be expected in an ordinary, average or normal boy of 15 as in an older person, are they to treat the lesser powers of self-control possessed by an ordinary, average or normal boy of 15 as the standard of self-control with which the conduct of the accused is to be compared?

In my opinion a proper direction to the jury on the question left to their exclusive determination by section 3 of the Act of 1957 would be on the following lines. The judge should state what the question is to them using the very words of the section. He should then explain to them that the reasonable man referred to in the question is a person having the power of self-control to be expected of an ordinary person of the sex and age of the accused, but in other respects sharing such of the accused's characteristics as they think would affect the gravity of the provocation to him; and that the question is not merely whether such a person would in like circumstances be provoked to lose self-control but also whether he would react to the provocation as the accused did.

It seems to me that as a result of the changes effected by section 3 a jury is fully entitled to consider whether an accused person, placed as he was, only acted as even a reasonable man might have acted if he had been in the accused's situation.

Read the two extracts above and answer the questions

Questions:

1. What are the three essential elements of a plea of provocation identified in s3 of the Homicide Act 1957?
2. What question does Lord Diplock say is the one that needs to be answered in the case of *Camplin*?
3. What does Lord Diplock suggest was the reason for including a 'reasonable man' test in the law on provocation?
4. Why does Lord Diplock say that the jury should be entitled to take into account characteristics of the accused?
5. In what way does Lord Diplock suggest that *Bedder* is wrong?
6. What is the appropriate test identified by Lord Diplock in *Camplin*?

Extract adapted from 'Battered Women and Provocation: The Implications of *R v Ahluwhalia*', Donald Nicolson and Robert Sanghvi, *Criminal Law Review*, October 1993, pp 728–738

Deepak Ahluwhalia began beating Kiranjit only days after their arranged marriage. Over the next decade, despite two restraining injunctions, his violence continued to increase in frequency and ferocity until it occurred almost daily. Kiranjit was slapped, punched, pushed when pregnant, beaten with hard objects, sexually abused and raped. Her many injuries included persistent bruising, broken bones and teeth, split and swollen lips, scalding and being knocked unconscious. Frequent death threats by Deepak, sometimes made while holding a foot-long screwdriver close to her, were lent credence by attempts at strangulation and running down.

From January 1989 the violence intensified. In March Kiranjit discovered Deepak was having an affair, exacerbating her worries over the future of their marriage. But when he left her for a few days, she abjectly pleaded for his return, making a number of self-denying promises. On his return the beatings continued.

On the night of May 8/9, 1989, Kiranjit begged Deepak not to desert the family, but he refused to talk to her, declaring that their relationship was over. He demanded money for a telephone bill and threatened to beat her the next morning if it was not forthcoming. Later he put a hot clothes iron against her face, threatening to burn her if she did not leave him alone. Deepak then went to bed. After brooding for about two-and-a-half hours, Kiranjit went outside, fetched some petrol, lit a candle, poured the petrol over Deepak and ignited it. She then calmly collected her son and left the house. Alerted neighbours reported her to be in a shocked state. Six days later, Deepak died from his burns.

At her trial for murder, Mrs Ahluwhalia denied having the requisite *mens rea* and pleaded provocation in the alternative. The jury was unimpressed and she began a life sentence ... she eventually obtained leave to appeal. Three grounds of appeal were argued. The first two alleged jury misdirections on the subjective and objective conditions of provocation, respectively, and the third that there was fresh evidence of diminished responsibility. On the latter ground alone, the Court of Appeal set aside Mrs Ahluwhalia's conviction as unsafe and unsatisfactory and ordered a retrial.

The treatment of the first ground of appeal has gone largely unnoticed, yet is perhaps the most important aspect of the case in challenging the law's maleness ... the subjective condition requires a 'sudden and temporary loss of self-control.'

Designation of the existence of a 'cooling time', not simply as evidence of cooled passion, but as legally precluding the provocation defence, was clearly premised upon a male-oriented view of behaviour and significantly prejudiced battered women.

On the objective condition of provocation, the trial judge had directed the jury to consider how a reasonable, educated, Asian woman would have responded to the provocation. The appellant argued that this wrongly omitted to mention that being a battered woman was also a relevant characteristic.

The decision in *Ahluwhalia* has been shown to provide some assistance to battered women who kill, but in a way which is likely to push them down the medical paths of diminished responsibility and Battered Woman Syndrome, both of which have invidious consequences for battered women and for women in general. Nevertheless, the decision does leave openings which can be exploited in less harmful ways.

First, the door left ajar by the Court of Appeal's treatment of the subjective condition of provocation can be forced open, by arguing for jury directions which do not treat a 'cooling time' as legally precluding the defence. This will obviously help battered defendants avoid life sentences. It should also encourage prosecutors to accept manslaughter pleas,

thus sparing the battered women the murder trial – an experience which could be described as the bruising which follows the battering. In addition, if the police learn as a matter of course to investigate not just the moment of the killing, but also its history, the credibility of a battered woman's evidence in her defence or mitigation will be bolstered by the spontaneity of her original confession.

Of course the biggest obstacle to battered women posed by provocation's subjective condition remains: the need to show that self-control was in fact lost. The man who 'snaps' following provocation can show that homicide was demonstrably a result of a sudden loss of self-control. Like Kiranjit Ahluwhalia, battered women frequently behave in an outwardly calm manner, suggesting revenge rather than rage. The next step is therefore to persuade the courts to accept that an outwardly calm killing by a battered woman is legally and morally the equivalent to the paradigmatic male 'snapping' since in neither case has reason 'dominion over the mind'.

Finally, the Court of Appeal's recognition of the relevance to provocation of the battered women context can be exploited in a way which avoids the problems of BWS. Instead of expecting jury members to consider how reasonable sufferers would have reacted to the provocation – itself absurdly unrealistic – judges can be asked to direct juries to simply consider how a reasonable person in the shoes of the defendant, having suffered the same level of violence and abuse, might have been expected to act.

Questions:

1. Why would Kiranjit Ahluwhalia's plea of provocation have failed?
2. Why is a 'cooling off period' or 'cooling time' so important in deciding whether there has been provocation?
3. Why do the authors suggest that the way in which a battered woman reacts to a provocation is the same as men 'snapping'?
4. What are the possible dangers in accepting this reasoning?
5. Is the attitude of the authors that the law on provocation is fairer to men than to women justified?
6. Why is a battered woman like Kiranjit Ahluwhalia succeeding under diminished responsibility but not under provocation unsatisfactory?

Extract adapted from 'Self control and the reasonable man', Laurence Toczek, *New Law Journal*, 11 August 2000

R v Smith [is] the most important case involving provocation in many years.

Provocation involves a consideration of two questions. The first, subjective question is whether the defendant was provoked to lose self-control. The second, objective question is whether the provocation was enough to make a reasonable man lose self-control and do as the defendant did.

The issue ... in *Smith* was the extent to which juries, when considering the second question, can take into account mental characteristics of a defendant which reduce his or her powers of self-control. By a majority of three to two, the House of Lords decided that such characteristics can be taken into account.

Smith [an alcoholic, who stabbed and killed a friend during an argument,] raised the defence of provocation [and] argued that the jury should be allowed to take into account the fact that, at the time of the killing, he was suffering from a severe depressive illness which reduced his powers of self-control.

[In the House of Lords] his conviction was quashed and a conviction for manslaughter substituted. Lord Hoffmann anticipate[d] potential objections ...

First [that] 'individual peculiarities which bear on the gravity of the provocation should be taken into account, whereas [those] bearing on the accused's level of self-control should not'.

Lord Hoffmann doubts the ability of jurors to perform such 'mental gymnastics'.

... second ... the argument that if there is no limit to the characteristics which can be taken into account, the objective element will disappear completely. Lord Hoffmann agrees that this would be most undesirable [so] suggests that judges should direct juries that 'characteristics such as jealousy and obsession should be ignored in relation to the objective element'. [He also refers] to juries being told that they 'may think that there was some characteristic of the accused, whether temporary or permanent, which affected the degree of control which society could reasonably have expected of *him* and which it would be unjust not to take into account.' Textbooks it seems will have to be rewritten.

Questions:

1. Laurence Toczek calls *Smith* 'the most important case involving provocation in many years'. Why do you think this is?
2. How does Lord Hoffmann justify changing the previous rule on characteristics?

 Try this sample A Level exam problem:

John's wife, Emily, has a reputation for being unfaithful. Colleagues at work, particularly his friend, Ian, often tease him about this. John also suffers from a depressive illness which means he tends to lose his temper quite easily. One evening, while Ian is at John's house, Emily comes home very late and begins to tell him about the enjoyable evening she has just had with her latest boyfriend. When John says that he does not want to hear this, Emily tells him that she does not love him. Ian tells John that he is a coward for not doing anything about it. John storms out of the room, saying that he is going to bed. Ian stays, talking to Emily. Two hours later, John comes downstairs and stabs both Ian and Emily with a kitchen knife, killing both of them.

4.3 Failed suicide pact

Extract from the Homicide Act 1957 (s4)

4. Suicide pacts

(1) It shall be manslaughter, and shall not be murder, for a person acting in pursuance of a suicide pact between him and another to kill the other or be a party to the other being killed by a third person.

(2) Where it is shown that a person charged with the murder of another killed the other or was a party to his being killed, it shall be for the defence to prove that the person charged was acting in pursuance of a suicide pact between him and the other.

(3) For the purposes of this section 'suicide pact' means a common agreement between two or more persons having for its object the death of all of them, whether or not each is to take his own life, but nothing done by a person who enters into a suicide pact shall be treated as done by him in pursuance of the pact unless it is done while he has the settled intention of dying in pursuance of the pact.

Questions:

1. Who has the burden of proving the existence of a suicide pact, and why do you think this is?
2. How many people could be involved?

Revision exercise:
WORDSEARCH: VOLUNTARY MANSLAUGHTER

Complete the Wordsearch below and you should find five words that are significant to voluntary manslaughter and five key cases.

They will be in a straight line but can be found running left to right or right to left, top to bottom or bottom to top, or diagonally up or down.

H	T	T	A	B	A	C	K	L	E
E	T	R	L	R	B	O	O	O	M
A	K	I	L	O	B	E	R	R	O
B	O	C	M	B	E	D	D	E	R
I	C	H	E	S	T	E	R	R	D
H	I	D	A	S	N	I	N	O	N
T	T	T	I	I	U	V	A	R	Y
C	S	I	C	K	E	N	M	B	S
A	I	D	E	N	I	B	E	T	E
P	R	I	P	P	O	W	L	C	F
E	E	H	M	A	D	U	B	A	I
D	T	A	A	P	A	Y	A	E	W
I	C	C	C	A	R	N	N	D	D
C	A	A	A	N	S	S	O	I	E
I	R	I	E	E	C	S	S	C	R
U	A	R	R	E	E	E	A	I	E
S	H	W	E	P	O	T	E	M	T
S	C	H	O	O	Z	I	R	O	T
A	I	L	A	H	W	U	L	H	A
B	I	L	L	H	A	B	L	O	B

CHAPTER 5

UNLAWFUL KILLING: INVOLUNTARY MANSLAUGHTER

Involuntary manslaughter involves any killing falling between murder and an accidental killing. The problems are easy to imagine, with such a vast area. Constructive manslaughter involves an unlawful act which is dangerous and which inadvertently causes death. It is also possible to have reckless manslaughter and, in situations where a duty is owed, gross negligence manslaughter is possible.

5.1 Constructive manslaughter

Extract adapted from the judgment in *R v Church* [1966] 1 QB 59

Facts

Church was mocked about his impotence by his female victim. He knocked her unconscious and, not being able to revive her, he panicked, thinking she was dead, and threw her into a river where she drowned. He was acquitted of murder but convicted of manslaughter. He appealed unsuccessfully on the direction of the trial judge on the requirements of manslaughter.

Judgment

EDMUND-DAVIES LJ:

Two passages in the summing up are here material. They are these: (1) 'If by an unlawful act of violence done deliberately to the person of another, that other is killed, the killing is manslaughter even though the accused never intended death or grievous bodily harm to result. If this woman was alive, as she was, when he threw her into the river, what he did was the deliberate act of throwing a living body into the river. That is an unlawful killing and it does not matter whether he believed she was dead or not, and that is my direction to you,' and (2) 'I would suggest to you, though it is of course for you to approach your task as you think fit, that a convenient way of approaching it would be to say: What do we think about this defence that he honestly believed the woman to be dead? If you think that it is true, why then, as I have told you, your proper verdict would be one of manslaughter, not murder.'

Such a direction is not lacking in authority... Nevertheless, in the judgment of this court it was a misdirection. It amounted to telling the jury that, whenever any unlawful act is committed in relation to a human being which resulted in death there must be, at least, a conviction for manslaughter. This might at one time have been regarded as good law ... it appears to this court that the passage of years has achieved a

transformation in this branch of the law and, even in relation to manslaughter, a degree of *mens rea* has become recognised as essential. To define it is a difficult task, and in *Andrews v DPP* Lord Atkin spoke of the 'element of "unlawfulness" which is the elusive factor.' Stressing that we are here leaving entirely out of account those ingredients of homicide which might justify a verdict of manslaughter on the grounds of (a) criminal negligence, or (b) provocation, or (c) diminished responsibility, the conclusion of this court is that an unlawful act causing the death of another cannot, simply because it is an unlawful act, render a manslaughter verdict inevitable. For such a verdict inexorably to follow, the unlawful act must be such as all sober and reasonable people would inevitably recognise must subject the other person to, at least, the risk of some harm resulting therefrom, albeit not serious harm.

If such be the test, as we judge it to be, then it follows that in our view it was a misdirection to tell the jury simpliciter that it mattered nothing for manslaughter whether or not the appellant believed Mrs Nott to be dead when he threw her in the river ... in the circumstances, such a misdirection does not, in our judgment, involve that the conviction for manslaughter must or should be quashed.

Extract adapted from the judgment in *DPP v Newbury and Jones* [1977] AC 500, HL

Facts

Two 15-year-old boys pushed a piece of concrete paving slab off a bridge, into the path of an oncoming train. The guard was then killed when the concrete slab hit him. The boys were convicted and appealed unsuccessfully to the Court of Appeal who certified the following point of general public importance: 'Can a defendant be properly convicted of manslaughter, when his mind is not affected by drink or drugs, if he did not foresee that his act might cause harm to another?'

Judgment

LORD SALMON:

The learned judge did not direct the jury that they should acquit the appellants unless they were satisfied beyond a reasonable doubt that the appellants had foreseen that they might cause harm to someone by pushing the piece of paving stone off the parapet into the path of the approaching train. In my view the learned judge was quite right not to give such a direction to the jury. The direction which he gave is completely in accordance with established law, which possibly with one exception, has never been challenged. In *Larkin* Humphreys J said:

> 'Where the act which a person is engaged in performing is unlawful, then if at the same time it is a dangerous act, that is, an act which is likely to injure another person, and quite inadvertently he causes the death of that other person by that act, then he is guilty of manslaughter.'

I agree entirely with Lawton LJ that that is an admirably clear statement of the law which has been applied many times. It makes it plain (a) that an accused is guilty of manslaughter if it is proved that he intentionally did an act which was unlawful and dangerous and that that act inadvertently caused death and (b) that it is unnecessary to prove that the accused knew that the act was unlawful or dangerous. This is one of the reasons why cases of manslaughter vary so infinitely in their gravity. They may amount to little more than pure inadvertence and sometimes to little less than murder.

The test is still the objective test. In judging whether the act was dangerous, the test is not did the accused recognise that it was dangerous but would all sober and reasonable people recognise its danger.

Extract adapted from the judgment in *R v Scarlett, New Law Journal Law Reports*, 30 July 1993

Facts

The appellant was licensee of a public house. Ten minutes after closing time one evening, a heavily built man the worse for drink entered the public house. The appellant told him that he would not serve him and told him to get out or he would put him out. The man then indicated that he was not going to leave voluntarily; the appellant then pinned his arms and bundled him to the door. He got him as far as the lobby, where the man fell backwards down a flight of five steps ... struck his head when he fell and received injuries from which he later died. The appellant was charged with manslaughter. The prosecution case was

that the appellant had used excessive force and thus committed an unlawful act because he had imparted such a momentum to the deceased that [his] fall was a consequence and his death was consequently manslaughter. The appellant was convicted. He appealed successfully.

Judgment

LORD BELDAM:

This unfortunate miscarriage of justice might have been avoided if the clear advice of the Criminal Law Revision Committee in 1980 had been implemented. That distinguished committee recommended abolition of the antiquated relic of involuntary manslaughter based on the commission of an unlawful act and the adoption of the more rational and systematic approach to the law of manslaughter they proposed. The present law is in urgent need of reform.

The judge began his summing up by telling [the jury] that the case boiled down to one fairly short question which they would have to ask themselves: 'Am I sure that [the appellant] used unnecessary and unreasonable and therefore unlawful force in ejecting [the deceased] and did that force actually cause his fall?' The whole tenor of the judge's directions was that if the jury concluded that the appellant used more force than was necessary in the circumstances, and if they were satisfied that that caused the deceased to fall and strike his head, he was guilty of manslaughter. His exposition that in law manslaughter was made out 'If the killing was the result of the accused man's unlawful act, like an assault which all reasonable people would inevitably realise must subject the victim to some form of harm even if not serious' was founded on the statement of the law in *DPP v Newbury*. The conduct of the accused in that case was clearly both unlawful and dangerous.

Where one of the issues for the jury is whether the accused is guilty of the unlawful act of assault in circumstances in which he is entitled to use reasonable force either in self-defence or for the purpose of preventing crime, or as here in removing a trespasser, the need for a careful direction was stressed by Lord Lane in *R v Gladstone Williams*: 'One starts off with the meaning of the word "assault". "Assault" in the context of this case, that is to say using the word as a convenient abbreviation for assault and battery, is an act by which the defendant intentionally or recklessly applies unlawful force to the complainant.'

The issue in *R v Williams* was whether the accused was entitled to be acquitted if he mistakenly believed that he was justified in using force. The court held that, even if the jury came to the conclusion that the mistake was an unreasonable one, if the defendant may genuinely have been labouring under it, he was entitled to rely upon it ... because he did not intend to apply unlawful force.

Where, as in the present case, an accused is justified in using some force and can only be guilty of an assault if the force used is excessive, the jury ought to be directed that he cannot be guilty of an assault unless the prosecution proved that he acted with the mental element necessary to constitute his action an assault, that is: 'that the defendant intentionally or recklessly applied force to the person of another'.

Further they should be directed that he is not to be found guilty merely because he intentionally or recklessly used force which they consider to have been excessive.

They ought not to convict him unless they are satisfied that the degree of force used was plainly more than was called for by the circumstances as he believed them to be and, provided the circumstances called for the degree of force used, he was not to be convicted even if his belief was unreasonable.

The expression used by the witnesses that the appellant 'bundled' the deceased towards the door certainly provided no basis for saying the appellant was reckless, nor by itself did it imply that the force used was excessive in the circumstances.

It is important to emphasise that the question whether the action of the appellant was unlawful and whether it was dangerous have to be considered separately.

Read the three extracts above and answer the questions

Questions:

1. What does Edmund-Davies LJ say is wrong with the direction of the trial judge in *Church*?
2. What does he suggest is a better definition of a manslaughter resulting from an unlawful act?
3. According to Lord Salmon in *Newbury and Jones*, then, what are the three necessary ingredients that must be proved in order to establish this type of manslaughter?
4. How should the dangerousness of the unlawful act be measured, according to Lord Salmon?
5. Why, according to Lord Beldam in *Scarlett*, should a jury not convict merely because they think that the defendant 'intentionally or recklessly used force that they consider to be excessive'?

5.2 Gross negligence manslaughter

Extract adapted from the judgment in *Adomako* [1995] 1 AC 171, HL

Facts

An anaesthetist was convicted when the patient in his care became disconnected from the oxygen supply during an operation and he failed to notice it for ten minutes, so that the patient eventually suffered a cardiac arrest and died.

Judgment

LORD MACKAY LC:
In my opinion the ordinary principles of the law of negligence apply to [see] whether or not the defendant has been in breach of a duty of care towards the victim who has died. If such a breach of duty is established the next question is whether that breach of duty has caused the death of the victim. If so, the jury must go on to consider whether that breach of duty should be categorised as gross negligence and therefore as a crime. This will depend on the seriousness of the breach of duty committed by the defendant in all the circumstances in which the defendant was placed when it occurred. The jury will have to consider whether the extent to which the defendant's conduct departed from the proper standard of care incumbent upon him, involving as it must have done a risk of death to the patient, was such that it should be judged criminal. It is true that to a certain extent this involves an element of circularity, but in this branch of the law I do not believe that is fatal to its being a correct test of how far conduct must depart from accepted standards to be characterised as criminal. This is necessarily a question of degree and an attempt to specify that degree more closely is I think likely to achieve only a spurious precision. The essence of the matter which is supremely a jury question is whether having regard to the risk of death involved, the conduct of the defendant was so bad in all the circumstances as to amount in their judgment to a criminal act or omission.

Extract adapted from 'Manslaughter, *mens rea* and medicine', Gary Slapper, *New Law Journal*, 8 July 1994

The combined effect of two recent developments may be to halt the apparently growing trend to prosecute negligent doctors for manslaughter when death results from their serious errors. The first development was the publication by the Crown Prosecution Service of its revised code, and the second was the House of Lords decision in *R v Adomako*.

It has been historically rare for doctors to be prosecuted for manslaughter following the death of a patient under their care, although, strangely, one of the main authorities on manslaughter is *R v Bateman*. Here a doctor performing a manual version (turning the baby's head downwards) during childbirth mistakenly removed a portion of the patient's uterus, ruptured her bladder and caused other internal injuries from which the patient died the following week.

The key change in the new code is the inclusion of public interest factors which may militate against a prosecution. In cases which pass the evidential test (that is, that there is sufficient admissible evidence to give the case a 'realistic prospect of conviction'), prosecutors must weigh up whether the public interest is best served by a prosecution.

Doctors are trained for and dedicated to preserving and improving life. The decision to spend thousands of pounds on prosecuting one for manslaughter should clearly be a very rare event. Doctors are increasingly working over-long hours and under huge, often unmanageable stress. Yet the Government has secured the exclusion of hospital doctors from the European Union's Working Time Directive, designed to prevent unhealthy working practices.

The House of Lords decision in *R v Adomako* should be seen as a clarification of law which lessens the likelihood of doctors being convicted of manslaughter. During the operation a disconnection occurred at the endotracheal tube connection. The supply of oxygen to the patient ceased and led ten minutes later to cardiac arrest. The patient was going blue, his chest was not moving and an alarm sounded on the blood pressure monitor but the appellant failed to notice or remedy the disconnection. The defendant's conviction for manslaughter was upheld but the test of 'gross negligence' was confirmed to be something, effectively, in the hands of the jury. Lord Mackay stated that the test of how far conduct must depart from accepted standards to be characterised as criminal was necessarily a question of degree. Any attempt to specify that degree more closely was likely to achieve only a spurious precision. The essence of the matter was 'supremely a jury question'; it was, whether, having regard to the risk involved, the conduct of the defendant was so bad in all the circumstances as to amount in their judgment to a criminal act or omission.

In the wake of the hospital league tables, and the current concern to evaluate medical care in a corporate way, it is to be hoped that jurors asked to decide whether a doctor has been criminally negligent will take into account the whole context including the situation in which the doctor was put to work by the employer.

Extract adapted from 'Medical manslaughter: why this shift from tort to crime?', Robert Wheeler, *New Law Journal*, 19 April 2002

The conventional remedy for the damaged patient was an action in negligence against the Health Authority. In the case of an apparently avoidable death due to a lapse in the duty of care, a dependant of the deceased could bring an action. However, in recent years, there have been several cases where the initial action has been criminal, for gross negligence manslaughter.

This seems to be counter-intuitive. The burden of proof is greater in criminal cases, making the outcome less certain. The hope for an apology diminishes and the financial reward is less.

… the corporate indemnity cover of the Trusts for whom they work now protects doctors. The plaintiff's success in winning substantial damages can no longer be regarded as punitive. The inability of the aggrieved to punish the doctor in a meaningful way means that [their] rights cannot be exercised, the accountability cannot be laid firmly at the door of the transgressor.

A prosecution in manslaughter changes all of that.

Therefore for the patient, the shift to manslaughter has given greater opportunity for revenge. Patients in general are increasingly encouraged to view this punitive process as fair.

In *R v Adomako* the House of Lords confirmed that Gross Negligence was the correct test. The focus was not on the mind of the defendant, but on his conduct and whether it failed to measure up to the objective standard set by the jury.

The jury therefore sets the standard. This makes the law uncertain, because the arbiter of fact is constantly changing. It was apparent in *Adomako* that Lord Mackay failed to distinguish between a risk of death and a risk to health and welfare, after which death ensues. What is the level of negligence required before a tort becomes a crime?

… the trial judge in *R v Singh (Gurphal)* [1999] Crim LR 582 directed that on a charge of gross negligence manslaughter 'the circumstances must be such that a reasonably prudent person would have foreseen a serious and obvious risk not merely of injury or even serious injury but of death.' The Law Commission identifies the problem: death as a result of a serious mistake by a doctor is in the same category as conduct falling only just short of murder, as well as minor assaults leading to death. The Commission has now recommended that the offence of 'killing by gross carelessness' be adopted in the Draft Involuntary Homicide Bill. ... the defendant is guilty of killing by gross carelessness if:

- A risk that his conduct will cause death or serious injury would be obvious to a reasonable person in his position;
- He is capable of appreciating that risk at the material time and either–
  (i) his conduct falls far below what can reasonably be expected of him in the circumstances; or
  (ii) he intends by his conduct to cause some injury or is aware of, and unreasonably takes, the risk that it may do so.

Although retaining the punitive element in cases reminiscent of the spirit of gross negligence, the shift from tort to crime is made less easy and may avoid criminalising doctors who make an error that might be made by a reasonable practitioner.

Read the three extracts above and answer the questions

Questions:

1. According to Lord Mackay, who should decide the test of whether the defendant's conduct amounted to gross negligence?
2. What does Lord Mackay think that the presence of gross negligence depends on?
3. In what way is the Crown Prosecution Service Code of Practice likely to affect prosecutions of doctors for manslaughter?
4. Why do you think that Gary Slapper thinks that to prosecute doctors for manslaughter is a bad thing?
5. In what way do you think that the case of *Adomako* will 'clarify' the law on manslaughter and make prosecution of doctors less likely?
6. In his article, what does Robert Wheeler see as the defects of the *Adomako* judgment?
7. How are the Law Commission proposals an improvement?

5.3 Reckless manslaughter

Extract adapted from the judgment in *R v Lidar* [2000] 4 Archbold News

Facts

Following an argument outside a club, the victim had reached in the window of the appellant's car, attacking his passenger. The appellant drove off and the victim's legs caught under the rear wheel and he was killed when the car ran over him. The appellant was acquitted of murder, convicted of manslaughter and appealed against sentence, claiming the judge was in error for failing to direct on gross negligence.

Judgment

EVANS LJ:

The [judge directed on] manslaughter: ' ... the Crown have to prove that the defendant acted recklessly. Recklessly in this context means that the defendant foresaw that some physical harm, however slight, might result to Kully from driving the car as he did and yet ignoring that risk he nevertheless went on to drive as he did. Mere inadvertence is not enough. The defendant must have been proved to have been indifferent to an obvious risk of injury ... or actually to have foreseen the risk but to have determined nevertheless to run it.'

In *Adomako* the House of Lords affirmed the characteristics of 'gross negligence' manslaughter and ... also held that juries might properly be directed in terms of recklessness although the precise definition derived from *Seymour* [1983] 2 AC 493 should no longer be used. Lord Mackay LC said this:

'I consider it perfectly appropriate that the word "reckless" be used in cases of involuntary manslaughter, but as Lord Atkin put it "in the ordinary connotation of that word." Examples in which this was done ... with complete accuracy are *Reg v Stone* [1977] QB 354 and *Reg v West London Coroner ex parte Gray* [1988] QB 467.... I entirely agree with the view that the circumstances to which a charge of involuntary manslaughter may apply are so various that it is unwise to attempt to categorise or detail specimen directions.'

Nothing here suggests that for the future 'recklessness' could no longer be a basis for proving the offence of manslaughter: rather, the opposite. *Smith & Hogan* records that 'For many years the courts have used the terms "recklessness" and "gross negligence" to describe the fault required for involuntary manslaughter ... without any clear definition of either term. It was not clear whether these terms were merely two ways of describing the same thing, or whether they represented two distinct conditions of fault'. After referring to *Adomako*, the learned author continues:

'Gross negligence is a sufficient, but not necessarily the only fault for manslaughter. To some extent manslaughter by overt recklessness, conscious risk-taking still survives.'

In our judgment, the judge was correct in his view that this was a case of 'reckless' manslaughter and to direct the jury accordingly. We reject the alternative submission that he was wrong not to direct the jury as to gross negligence manslaughter, whether in place of or in substitution for the direction as to recklessness. Indeed, in a case such as the present, we find it difficult to understand how the point of criminal liability can be reached, where gross negligence is alleged, without identifying the point by reference to the concept of recklessness as it is commonly understood: that is to say, whether the driver of the motor vehicle was aware of the necessary degree of risk of serious injury to the victim and nevertheless chose to disregard it, or was indifferent to it. If the gross negligence direction had been given, the recklessness direction would still have been necessary. The recklessness direction in fact given made the gross negligence direction superfluous and unnecessary.

Questions:

1. According to the trial judge in *Lidar*, how is recklessness to be measured?
2. According to Lord Justice Evans, how is this consistent with the judgment of Lord Mackay in *Adomako*?
3. What is the criticism made by Smith and Hogan of the use of gross negligence and recklessness in manslaughter?
4. In what ways was the trial judge's direction correct, according to Lord Justice Evans?
5. To what extent do you think that the decision in *Lidar* has helped to make the law on manslaughter more sensible?

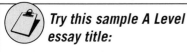

Try this sample A Level essay title:

'Involuntary manslaughter is an offence of ill-defined boundaries covering the middle ground between murder and accidental death.'

Discuss the validity of this statement.

Revision exercises:
MISSING LINKS

In each of the following short statements, fill in the missing words to complete the passages accurately.

1. Manslaughter can occur in one of two ways. If .... could be charged but the defendant can claim one of three partial defences identified in the .... Act 19..., then the charge may be reduced to manslaughter and a full range of .... will be available rather than the mandatory 'life' as for murder. This is then known as .... manslaughter. Manslaughter on the other hand can be classed as .... This is where there is insufficient .... to charge the defendant with murder.
2. .... manslaughter occurs in one of two ways. It could involve .... which is when a person owing a ...... falls so far below the standard expected of them that it goes beyond mere .... and amounts to a crime. Alternatively .... manslaughter involves an inadvertent killing caused while carrying out an .... act which is also ....
3. .... manslaughter at one stage was measured .... according to cases such as *Seymour* and .... Now, however, ... recklessness will apply and so the recklessness will be measured ....

CHAPTER 6

NON-FATAL OFFENCES AGAINST THE PERSON: ASSAULTS

Assaults are mentioned in the Criminal Justice Act 1988 and also in the Offences Against the Person Act 1861. The law is very inconsistent and in need of reform. Particular problems concern the necessary *mens rea* for the offence and the situations in which consent is available as a defence.

6.1 Common assault (assault and battery)

Extract adapted from the judgment in *Smith v Chief Superintendent of Woking Police Station* (1983) 76 Cr App Rep 234, DC

Facts

The defendant entered the grounds of the house where the victim lived and looked in through her bed-sit window. The victim saw him and, it was accepted, was then terrified for days afterwards. It was also shown that the defendant intended to frighten his victim. The defendant appealed unsuccessfully against his conviction for assault.

Judgment

KERR LJ:

... the defendant intended to frighten Miss Mooney and Miss Mooney was frightened ... there is no need for a finding that what she was frightened of, which she probably could not analyse at that moment, was some innominate terror of some potential violence. It was clearly a situation where the basis of the fear ... was that she did not know what the defendant was going to do next, but that, whatever he might be going to do next, ... was something of a violent nature ... the justices ... were perfectly entitled to convict the defendant who had gone there, as they found, with the intention of frightening her and causing to her fear of some act of immediate violence, and therefore with the intention of committing an assault upon her.

Extract adapted from the judgment in *Collins v Wilcock* [1984] 1 WLR 1172

Facts

A policewoman took hold of a prostitute's arm to stop her walking away, but without having arrested her. The prostitute then scratched the policewoman's arm and was later convicted of assault. She successfully appealed on the ground that the policewoman was not lawfully carrying out her duty and so committed a battery.

Judgment

ROBERT GOFF LJ:

We are here primarily concerned with battery. The fundamental principle, plain and incontestable, is that every person's body is inviolate. It has long been established that any touching of another person, however slight, might amount to a battery. The effect is that everybody is protected not only against physical injury but against any form of physical molestation.

But so widely drawn a principle must inevitably be subject to some exceptions. For example, ... people may be subjected to the lawful exercise of the power of arrest; and reasonable force may be used in self-defence ... Generally speaking, consent is a defence to battery; and most of the physical contacts of everyday life are not battery because they are impliedly consented to ... Among such forms of conduct long held to be acceptable is touching a person for the purpose of engaging his attention ... A police officer may wish to engage a man's attention ... to question him. But if ... his use of physical contact in the face of non-cooperation persists beyond generally accepted standards of conduct, his action will become unlawful; and if a police officer restrains a man, for example by gripping his arm or his shoulder, then his action will also be unlawful, unless he is lawfully exercising his powers of arrest.

... the respondent took hold of the appellant by the left arm to restrain her. She was not proceeding to her arrest ... her action constituted a battery ... and was therefore unlawful. ... the appeal must be allowed ...

6.2 Actual bodily harm

Extract adapted from the judgment in *R v Venna* [1975] 3 WLR 737, CA

Facts

Venna was convicted of an assault contrary to s47 Offences Against the Person Act 1861. He had struggled with policemen trying to arrest him and had kicked one of them, fracturing that officer's hand. He appealed unsuccessfully against the trial judge's direction that he could be convicted if he intentionally kicked out or did so recklessly.

Judgment

JAMES LJ:

In *Fagan v Metropolitan Police Commissioner*, it was said: 'An assault is any act which intentionally or possibly recklessly causes another person to apprehend immediate and unlawful personal violence'. In *Fagan* it was not necessary to decide the question whether proof of recklessness is sufficient to establish the *mens rea* ingredient of assault. That question falls for decision in the present case. Why it was necessary for the Crown to put the case forward on the alternative bases of 'intention' and 'recklessness' is not clear to us.

On the evidence of the appellant himself, one would have thought that the inescapable inference was that the appellant intended to make physical contact with whoever might try to restrain him. Be that as it may, in the light of the direction given, the verdict may have been arrived at on the basis of 'recklessness'. Counsel for the appellant cited *Ackroyd v Barett* in support of his argument that recklessness, which falls short of intention, is not enough to support a charge of battery.

We see no reason in logic or in law why a person who recklessly applies physical force to the person of another should be outside the criminal law of assault. In many cases the dividing line between recklessness and intention is barely distinguishable. This is such a case.

Extract adapted from the judgment in *R v Ireland; R v Burstow*, House of Lords, *New Law Journal* Reports, 5 September 1997

Facts

I appealed from the dismissal of his appeal from the Court of Appeal against conviction on three counts of assault occasioning actual bodily harm contrary to s47 of the Offences against the Person Act 1861. The Court of Appeal certified as being a point of law of general public importance the question 'as to whether the making of a series of silent telephone calls can amount in law to an assault'. [This was the behaviour that led to I's conviction.]

B appealed against the dismissal by the Court of Appeal of his appeal against conviction [of] unlawfully and maliciously inflicting grievous bodily harm contrary to s20 of the 1861 Act following a ruling by the judge that an offence might be committed where no physical violence had been applied directly or indirectly to the body of the victim. [B had carried out an eight-month campaign of harassment against a woman, including both silent and abusive phone calls].

Judgment

LORD STEYN:

Harassment of women by repeated silent telephone calls, accompanied on occasions by heavy breathing, is apparently a significant social problem. That the criminal law should be able to deal with this problem, and so far as is practicable, afford effective protection to victims is self evident.

It is to the provisions of the Offences against the Person Act 1861 that one must turn to examine whether our law provides effective criminal sanctions for this type of case.

An ingredient of each of the offences is 'bodily harm' to a person. In respect of each section the threshold question is therefore whether a psychiatric illness, as testified to by a psychiatrist, can amount to 'bodily harm'. If ... the answer to the question is yes, it will be necessary to consider whether the persistent silent caller, who terrifies his victim and causes her to suffer a psychiatric illness, can be criminally liable ...

The correct approach is simply to consider whether the words of the 1861 Act considered in the light of contemporary knowledge cover a recognisable psychiatric injury ... .

The proposition that the Victorian legislator when enacting ss 18, 20 and 47 of the 1861 Act, would not have had in mind psychiatric illness is no doubt correct. Psychiatry was in its infancy. But the subjective intention of the draftsman is immaterial. The only relevant inquiry is as to the sense of the words in the context in which they are used.

[Accordingly] 'bodily harm' must be interpreted so as to include recognisable psychiatric illness.

[In] *Burstow* ... counsel laid stress on the difference between 'causing' grievous bodily harm in s18 and 'inflicting' grievous bodily harm in s20 [and] submitted that it is inherent in the word 'inflict' that there must be a direct or indirect application of force to the body ...

...The question is whether as a matter of current usage the contextual interpretation of 'inflict' can embrace the idea of one person inflicting psychiatric injury on another. One can without straining the language in any way answer ... in the affirmative ...

... It is now necessary to consider whether the making of silent telephone calls causing psychiatric injury is capable of constituting an assault under s47...

It is necessary to consider the two forms which an assault may take. The first is battery, which involves the unlawful application of force ... The second form of assault is an act causing the victim to apprehend an immediate application of force upon her ...

The proposition that a gesture may amount to an assault, but that words can never suffice, is unrealistic and indefensible ... There is no reason why something said should be incapable of causing an apprehension of immediate personal violence ... I would, therefore, reject the proposition that an assault can never be committed by words.

That brings me to the critical question whether a silent caller may be guilty of an assault. The answer to this question seems to me to be 'yes, depending on the facts'. It depends on questions of fact within the province of the jury. After all, there is no reason why a telephone caller who says to a woman in a menacing way 'I will be at your door in a minute or two' may not be guilty of an assault if he causes his victim to apprehend immediate personal violence. Take now the case of the silent caller. He intends by his silence to cause fear and so he is understood. The victim ... may fear the *possibility* of immediate personal violence. As a matter of law the caller may be guilty of an assault, whether he is or not will depend on the circumstance and in particular on the impact of the caller's potentially menacing call or calls on the victim. Such a prosecution case under s47 may be fit to leave to the jury. I conclude that an assault may be committed in the particular factual circumstances which I have envisaged. For this reason I reject the submission that as a matter of law a silent telephone caller cannot ever be guilty of an offence under s47.

Read the four extracts in the above two sections and answer the questions

Questions:

1. What are the simple elements of a common assault, as identified in *Smith v Chief Superintendent of Woking Police Station*?
2. What are the essential elements of a battery, according to *Collins v Wilcock*?
3. What exceptions does Goff LJ recognise in *Collins v Wilcock* justifying battery, and why do they not apply to the police officer in the case?
4. According to Lord Justice James in *Venna*, what does an accused have to do to commit assault?
5. Why is recklessness sufficient *mens rea* for assault?
6. In *Ireland and Burstow*, how does Lord Steyn suggest that the accused is able to be convicted for causing 'actual bodily harm'?
7. Also in *Ireland and Burstow*, what justification does Lord Steyn give for holding that words alone or even silence are sufficient for an assault?

6.3 Consent

Extract adapted from 'Consent: public policy or legal moralism?', Susan Nash, *New Law Journal*, 15 March 1996

In *R v Wilson* the Court of Appeal held that consensual activity between a husband and wife in the privacy of the matrimonial home was not a proper matter for a criminal prosecution. The defendant had been charged with assault occasioning actual bodily harm, contrary to s47 of the Offences Against the Person Act 1861. The 'activity' involved the defendant burning his initials onto his wife's right buttock with a hot knife because 'she had wanted his name on her body'. This decision rekindles the debate regarding the extent to which the criminal law should be concerned with the consensual activities of adults in private. In *R v Brown* the House of Lords upheld convictions under ss20 and 47 of the Offences Against the Person Act notwithstanding that the victims had given their consent. This decision has been described as 'unprincipled and incoherent'.

The trial judge in *Wilson* had ruled that consent was no defence to an assault occasioning actual bodily harm. In arriving at this conclusion he stated that he felt bound by *R v Donovan* and *R v Brown*. The Court of Appeal considered it misdirection for the judge to say these cases constrained him to rule that consent was no defence.

The majority of the House of Lords in *Brown* held that it was not in the public interest that a person should wound or cause actual bodily harm to another for no good reason. Thus, in the absence of a good reason the victim's consent would not amount to a defence to a charge under s47 or s20 of the 1861 Act.

The defendants had taken part in consensual acts of violence for the purpose of sexual gratification which had resulted in varying degrees of injury. The court was of the opinion that the satisfying of sado-masochistic desires could not be classed as a good reason and dismissed the appeals. Lord Templeman considered that in some circumstances the accused would be entitled to an acquittal although the activity resulted in the infliction of some injury.

'Surgery involves intentional violence resulting in actual or sometimes serious bodily harm but surgery is a lawful activity. Other activities carried on with consent by or on behalf of the injured person have been accepted as lawful notwithstanding that they involve actual bodily harm or may cause serious harm. Ritual circumcision, tattooing, ear-piercing and violent sports including boxing are lawful activities.' This reference to tattooing has now assumed significance. Lords Templeman and Jauncey referred to it as being an activity which, if carried out with the consent of an adult, did not involve an offence under s47. Wilson had been engaged in an activity which in principle was no more dangerous than professional tattooing. Thus, the Court of Appeal was of the opinion that it was not in the public interest that his activities should amount to criminal behaviour.

The Court of Appeal has now declared that *Brown* is not authority for the proposition that consent is no defence to a charge under s47 of the 1861 Act *in all circumstances* where actual bodily harm is deliberately inflicted upon a person. Public policy and public interest considerations will become increasingly important in deciding whether it is appropriate to criminalise consensual activity, giving rise to even greater uncertainty in the area.

Extract adapted from the judgment in *R v Coney* [1882] 8 QBD 534

Facts
Spectators at an illegal prize-fight were convicted of aiding and abetting the fight, though there was no evidence that they encouraged the fighters. The case

was then referred to the Court for Crown Cases Reserved where the convictions were quashed, as mere presence at the fight was insufficient for liability as an accessory. The court also considered whether the fighters were committing assaults, since they had consented to the fight.

Judgment

STEPHEN J:
The principle as to consent seems to me to be this: when one person is indicted for inflicting personal injury upon another, the consent of the person who sustains the injury is no defence to the person who inflicts the injury, if the injury is of such a nature, or is inflicted under such circumstances, that its infliction is injurious to the public as well as to the person injured. But the injuries given and received in prize-fights are injurious to the public, both because it is against the public interest that the lives and the health of the combatants should be endangered by blows, and because prize-fights are disorderly exhibitions, mischievous on many obvious grounds. Therefore the consent of the parties to the blows which they mutually receive does not prevent those blows from being assaults.

Extract adapted from the judgment in *R v Donovan* [1934] 2 KB 498, Court of Criminal Appeal

Facts
Donovan was convicted of common assault after caning a 17-year-old girl for sexual gratification. His defence that she consented was rejected. The conviction was quashed on appeal for a misdirection that it was for the Crown to disprove consent.

Judgment

SWIFT J:
If an act is unlawful in the sense of being in itself a criminal act, it is plain that it cannot be rendered lawful because the person to whose detriment it is done consents to it. No person can license another to commit a crime. So far as the criminal law is concerned, therefore, where the act charged is in itself unlawful, it can never be necessary to prove absence of consent on the part of the person wronged in order to obtain the conviction of the wrongdoer. There are, however, many acts in themselves harmless and lawful which become unlawful only if they are done without the consent of the person affected. What is, in one case, an innocent act of familiarity or affection, may, in another, be an assault, for no other reason than that, in the one case there is consent, and in the other consent is absent. As a general rule, although it is a rule to

which there are well-established exceptions, it is an unlawful act to beat another person with such a degree of violence that the infliction of bodily harm is a probable consequence, and when such an act is proved consent is immaterial.

Extract adapted from 'Inflicting injuries for sexual pleasure illegal, Lords rule', Frances Gibb, *The Times*, Friday, 12 March 1993

People who inflict sado-masochistic injuries on each other for sexual pleasure are guilty of criminal assault even though they consent to what happens, the law lords held yesterday.

In a landmark ruling which was immediately attacked by civil libertarians, the law lords held that consent to such practices was no defence to charges of wounding or causing actual bodily harm.

Lord Templeman said: 'Society is entitled and bound to protect itself against a cult of violence. Pleasure derived from the infliction of pain is an evil thing. Cruelty is uncivilised.'

The ruling prompted calls for a law on privacy. Andrew Puddephatt, general secretary of Liberty, said the ruling had 'potentially criminalised a whole range of perfectly harmless activities'.

Nicki Wolf, of Feminists Against Censorship, said the ruling showed 'Despite 30 years of campaigning to have domestic violence put on the political agenda, it seems legal condemnation is reserved for men who mutually consent to sado-masochistic sex.' She said the ruling was 'an insult to all women and we condemn it both for its removal of rights over our own bodies and the failure of the law to recognise the true nature of sexual violence'.

Lord Templeman said some consensual activities which involved actual bodily harm – such as ritual circumcision, tattooing, ear-piercing and violent sports like boxing – were lawful. But duelling and fighting were both unlawful and the consent of the protagonists afforded no defence.

He said there was a difference between violence which was incidental and violence which was inflicted for the indulgence of cruelty.

Read the three extracts above and answer the questions

Questions:

1. According to Susan Nash's article, when will consent be a defence to charges of assault and when will it not?
2. To what extent are these differences sensible or justifiable?
3. Why does the judge in *Coney* think that the defence of consent should not be available in the case of prize-fighting?
4. In what circumstances does the judge in *Donovan* suggest that consent cannot be available as a defence?
5. In what ways does the judgment in *Donovan* suggest that it is possible legally to inflict some physical harm on another person?
6. What different viewpoints are expressed in Frances Gibb's article regarding the inflicting of harm on other people?
7. In what circumstances do you think that a defence of consent can be justified in relation to assaults and wounding?

Revision exercises:
QUICK QUIZ: Cases

Below are 10 case names. In the middle column, tick if you can find them in this chapter. In the third column, if you do not think they are in this chapter, see if you can identify the number of the chapter(s) in which they appear.

Donovan		
Camplin		
Coney		
Brown		
Burstow		
Byrne		
Bratty		
Fagan		
Wilson		
Mowatt		

Guess the case!

Fig 6.1

Wounding offences are found in the Offences Against the Person Act 1861. They are even more in need of reform than assault offences. Inconsistencies include the use of different words in the different offences, 'cause' and 'inflict', which make it hard to differentiate a proper hierarchical structure to the offences. Problems also surround what *mens rea* is appropriate. There is also the problem of whether the offences must involve assaults or not.

7.1 Malicious wounding or GBH under s20 OAPA 1861

Extract from the Offences Against the Person Act 1861 (s20)

20. Inflicting bodily injury, with or without weapon

Whosoever shall unlawfully and maliciously wound or inflict any grievous bodily harm upon any other person, either with or without any weapon or instrument, shall be guilty of a misdemeanour, and being convicted thereof shall be liable to be kept in penal servitude [for not more than five years]

Extract adapted from *R v Martin* [1881] 8 QBD 54

Facts

Martin barred the exits to a theatre and then turned lights off in a staircase where many people would be exiting at the end of a performance. He did so to cause terror in the minds of the audience and succeeded in that end; many people were injured as a result. He was convicted, under s20, of unlawfully and maliciously inflicting grievous bodily harm and his appeal on the meaning of 'malicious' was unsuccessful.

Judgment

LORD COLERIDGE CJ:
Upon these facts the prisoner was convicted and the jury found all that was necessary to sustain the conviction. The prisoner must be taken to have intended the natural consequences of that which he did. He acted 'unlawfully and maliciously', not that he had any personal malice against the particular individuals injured, but in the sense of doing an unlawful act calculated to injure, and by which others were in fact injured. Just as in the case of a man who

unlawfully fires a gun among a crowd, it is murder if one of the crowd is thereby killed.

Extract adapted from the judgment in *R v Clarence* [1888] 2 QBD 23

Facts

The appellant had sexual intercourse with his wife, without telling her that he had venereal disease, and thereby infected her with the disease. He was convicted of offences under both s20 and s47 of the Offences Against the Person Act 1861. His appeal to the Court of Crown Cases Reserved succeeded because of the wife's consent to the intercourse. The court also considered the issue of whether or not an assault is necessary for a conviction under s20.

Judgment

STEPHEN J:
The question in this case is whether a man who knows that he has gonorrhoea, and who by having connection with his wife, who does not know it, infects her, is or is not guilty of an offence under either section 20 or section 47 of the Act.

If the present conviction is right it is clear that unless some distinction can be pointed out which does not occur to me, the sections must be held to apply, not only to venereal diseases, but to infection of every kind which is in fact communicated by one person to another by any act likely to produce it.

Not only is there no general principle which makes the communication of infection criminal, but such authority as exists is opposed to such a doctrine in relation to any disease.

I now come to the precise words of the statute.

Section 20 punishes 'every one who unlawfully and maliciously wounds or inflicts any grievous bodily harm upon any person either with or without any weapon or instrument'. Is there an 'infliction of bodily harm either with or without any weapon or instrument'? I think there is not.

The words appear to me to mean the direct causing of some grievous injury to the body itself with a weapon, as by a cut from a knife, or without a weapon, as by a blow with the fist, or by pushing a person down. Indeed though the word 'assault' is not used in the section, I think the words imply an assault and battery of which a wound or grievous bodily harm is the manifest immediate and obvious result. This is supported by *R v Taylor*, in which it was held that a prisoner could upon an indictment under that section be convicted of a common assault, because each offence, 'wounding' and 'inflicting grievous bodily harm' 'necessarily includes an assault,' though the word does not appear in the section.

Extract adapted from the judgment in *JCC (a minor) v Eisenhower* [1983] 3 All ER 230, QBD

Facts

The appellant had fired an air gun in the direction of the victim who had been struck in the area of the left eye, which had then caused a bruise under the eyebrow and some bleeding behind the eye. The appellant had been convicted under s20 Offences Against the Person Act 1861, and appealed successfully on the ground that the injuries were insufficient to amount to a 'wounding'.

Judgment

ROBERT GOFF LJ:
In my judgment, that conclusion (of the magistrates) was not in accordance with the law. It is not enough that there has been a rupturing of blood vessels internally for there to be a wound under the statute because it is impossible for a court to conclude from that evidence alone whether or not there has been any break in the continuity of the whole skin. There may have simply been internal bleeding of some kind or another, the cause of which is not established. Furthermore, even of there had been a break in some internal skin, there may not have been a break in the whole skin.

In these circumstances, the evidence is not enough, in my judgment, to establish a wound within the statute. In my judgment, the magistrates erred in their conclusion on the evidence before them.

Read the four extracts above and answer the questions

Questions:

1. According to the first three sources, what exactly is the meaning of the word 'maliciously'?
2. According to *Clarence,* what exactly does 'inflict' mean?
3. According to *Eisenhower,* what does 'wound' mean?

7.2 Wounding with intent or GBH under s18 OAPA 1861

Extract from the Offences Against the Person Act 1861 (s18)

18. Shooting or attempting to shoot, or wounding, with intent to do grievous bodily harm, or to resist apprehension

Whosoever shall unlawfully and maliciously by any means whatsoever wound or cause grievous bodily harm to any person with intent to do some grievous bodily harm to any person, or with intent to resist or prevent the lawful apprehension or detainer of nay person, shall be guilty of felony, and being convicted thereof shall be liable to be kept in penal servitude for life.

Extract adapted from the judgment in *R v Mowatt* [1967] 3 WLR 1192, CA

Facts

The defendant or his friend had stolen £5 from the victim's pocket. The victim seized hold of him and Mowatt then struck the victim, arguing that he was acting in self-defence. The defendant punched the victim and pulled him up from the ground, hitting him repeatedly until he nearly lost consciousness. He was charged with wounding with intent under s18 Offences Against the Person Act 1861 and convicted of s20 malicious wounding. He appealed unsuccessfully on the ground that the jury had not been properly directed on the meaning of the word 'maliciously'.

Judgment

DIPLOCK LJ:
In s18 the word 'maliciously' adds nothing. The intent expressly required by that section is more specific than

such element of foresight of consequences as is implicit in the word 'maliciously' and in directing a jury about an offence under this section the word 'maliciously' is best ignored. In the offence under s20 and in the alternative verdict which may be given on a charge under s18 – for neither of which is any specific intent required – the word 'maliciously' does import on the part of the person who unlawfully inflicts the wound or other grievous bodily harm an awareness that his act may have the consequences of causing some physical harm to some other person. That is what is meant by 'the particular kind of harm' in the citation from Professor Kenny's *Outlines of Criminal Law*. It is quite unnecessary that the accused should have foreseen that his unlawful act might cause physical harm of the gravity described in the section i.e. a wound or serious physical injury. It is enough that he should have foreseen that some physical harm to some person, albeit of a minor character, might result.

Extract adapted from Home Office, 'Violence: Reforming the Offences Against the Person Act 1861, Draft Offences Against the Person Bill 1998'

1(1) A person is guilty of an offence if he intentionally causes serious injury to another. (Max: Life imprisonment)

2(1) A person is guilty of an offence if he recklessly causes serious injury to another. (Max: seven years' imprisonment)

3(1) A person is guilty of an offence if he intentionally or recklessly causes injury to another. (Max: five years' imprisonment)

4(1) A person is guilty of an offence if–
  (a) he intentionally or recklessly applies force to or causes an impact on the body of another, or
  (b) he intentionally or recklessly causes the other to believe that any such force or impact is imminent.

(2) No such offence is committed if the force or impact, not being intended or likely to cause injury, is in the circumstances such as is generally acceptable in the ordinary conduct of daily life and the defendant does not know or believe that it is in fact unacceptable to the other person. (Max: six months' imprisonment)

15(1) In this Act 'injury' means–
  (a) physical injury, or
  (b) mental injury.

(2) Physical injury does not include anything caused by disease but (subject to that) it includes pain, unconsciousness and any other impairment of a person's physical condition.

(3) Mental injury does not include anything caused by disease but (subject to that) it includes any impairment of a person's mental health.

Read the three extracts above and answer the questions

Questions:

1. On reading s18 and s20, what appear to be the significant differences between them?
2. According to Coleridge, in *Martin*, what do the words 'unlawfully and maliciously' refer to in s20?
3. What does the case of *Clarence* tell us about the character of assaults as they occur in s20?
4. What will and will not amount to a wound, according to the judgment in *JCC v Eisenhower*?
5. How does Diplock LJ explain the different applications of the word 'malicious' in s18 and s20?
6. In what ways do you think that the wording in the offences identified in the Draft Offences Against the Person Bill 1998 will improve on the wording in the existing offences in the 1861 Act?

Try this sample A Level exam essay:

Consider why the courts will allow the defence of consent in certain circumstances and not in others.

Revision exercises:
MISSING LINKS

Checklist on ways of committing s20 or s18 Offences Against the Person Act 1861

Fill in the gaps in the checklist below:

s20 OAPA 1861

Either:
1. Unlawfully and .... wounds; or
2. .... and maliciously .... Grievous bodily harm with or without ....

s18 OAPA 1861

Either:
1. Unlawfully and .... wounds with intent to ... .
2. .... and maliciously .... with intent to resist ....
3. Unlawfully and maliciously .... grievous bodily harm with intent to ....

CHAPTER 8

PROPERTY OFFENCES: THEFT

Theft was codified in the 1968 Act but problems of interpretation meant that Parliament had to go back and pass a further Act in 1978. There are still problems of interpretation particularly with the meaning of 'appropriates'. There is an apparent overlap with the offence of deception in s15. The way that dishonesty is measured is also less than satisfactory.

Dishonesty

Extract from the Theft Act 1968 (s2)

2. 'Dishonesty'

(1) A person's appropriation of property belonging to another is not to be regarded as dishonest –
  (a) if he appropriates the property in the belief that he has in law the right to deprive the other of it, on behalf of himself or of a third person; or
  (b) if he appropriates the property in the belief that he would have the other's consent if the other knew of the appropriation and the circumstances of it; or
  (c) (except where the property came to him as trustee or personal representative) if he appropriates the property in the belief that the person to whom the property belongs cannot be discovered by taking reasonable steps.
(2) A person's appropriation of property belonging to another may be dishonest notwithstanding that he is willing to pay for the property.

Extract adapted from the judgment in *R v Ghosh* [1982] 3 WLR 110

Facts

The defendant, a surgeon acting as a *locum,* was convicted of deception for falsely representing that he had carried out an abortion, which he had not, and claiming the money for the operation, when it had in fact been carried out by another doctor under the National Health Service. He argued that the fees were in any case owed to him as consultancy fees and that, therefore, his actions were not dishonest. He appealed unsuccessfully on the ground of a misdirection on the meaning of 'dishonesty'.

Judgment

LORD LANE CJ:
Is 'dishonesty' in s1 of the Theft Act 1968 intended to characterise a course of conduct? Or is it intended to describe a state of mind? If the former, then we can well understand that it could be established independently of the knowledge or belief of the accused. But if, as we think, it is the latter, then the knowledge and belief of the accused are at the root of the problem.

Take for example a man who comes from a country where public transport is free. On his first day here he travels on a bus. He gets off without paying. He never had any intention of paying. His mind is clearly honest; but his conduct, judged objectively by what he has done, is dishonest. It seems to us that in using the word 'dishonesty' in the Theft Act, Parliament cannot have intended to catch dishonest conduct in this sense ...

If we are right that dishonesty is something in the mind of the accused, then if the mind of the accused is honest, it cannot be deemed dishonest merely because members of the jury would have regarded it as dishonest to embark on that course of conduct.

There remains the objection that to adopt a subjective test is to abandon all standards but that of the accused himself, and to bring about a state of affairs in which 'Robin Hood would be no robber'. This misunderstands the nature of the subjective test. [The defendant] is entitled to say 'I did not know that anybody would regard what I was doing as dishonest.' He may not be believed ... But if he is believed, the jury cannot be sure that he was dishonest.

In determining whether the prosecution has proved that the defendant was acting dishonestly, a jury must first of all decide whether according to the ordinary standards of reasonable and honest people what was done was dishonest. If it was not dishonest by those standards, that is the end of the matter and the prosecution fails.

If it was dishonest by those standards, then the jury must consider whether the defendant himself must have realised that what he was doing was by those standards dishonest.

Read the two extracts above and answer the questions

Questions:

1. What is unsatisfactory about the definitions of 'dishonesty' in s2 Theft Act 1968?
2. What is the objective part of Lord Lane's test in *Ghosh*?
3. What is the subjective part of the test in *Ghosh*?
4. What problems is the test likely to cause?

Try this sample A Level exam problem:

Using the test in *Ghosh* and the tests of dishonesty in s2, consider whether there is dishonesty in the following situations:

(a) John gets on a train and picks up and starts to read a newspaper that has been left on the seat he occupies. After the train moves off, Reginald returns from the buffet and demands to know what John is doing with his newspaper.

(b) Aaron regularly borrows his next-door neighbour's lawnmower. He takes it out of the next-door shed when his neighbour is on holiday and uses it but forgets to put it back.

(c) As a hard-working law lecturer, I take books from the college library to help with my preparation and with no intention of returning them because I honestly believe that the college should supply me with books.

(d) The garage has repaired Jim's car. Jim does not like the bill and refuses to pay, so the garage will not let him take the car back. When the garage is shut, he returns with his spare keys and takes the car back, believing that the garage had no right to keep the car.

Appropriation

Extract from the Theft Act 1968 (s3)

3. 'Appropriates'

(1) Any assumption by a person of the rights of an owner amounts to an appropriation, and this includes, where he has come by the property (innocently or not) without stealing it, any later assumption of a right to it by keeping or dealing with it as owner.

Extract adapted from '*Gomez* revisited' Richard Akinjide, *New Law Journal*, 10 June 1994

In *R v Gomez*, the House of Lords finally decided that *Lawrence* was rightly decided and that *Morris* was wrongly decided.

Both were previous decisions of the House of Lords. The resolution, at last, is therefore of great importance, but Lord Lowry delivered a powerful dissenting judgment.

The Court of Appeal ... granted a certificate that a point of law of general public importance was involved ... to wit:

'When theft is alleged and that which is alleged to be stolen passes to the defendant with the consent of the owner, but that consent has been obtained by a false representation, has: (a) an appropriation within the meaning of s1(1) of the Theft Act 1968 taken place, or (b) must such passing of property necessarily involve an element of adverse interference with or usurpation of some right of the owner?'

The House of Lords allowed the appeal by the Crown and restored the conviction of Gomez after answering the two questions as follows: (a) Yes, and (b) No.

Gomez, an assistant to the manager of a shop, induced his manager to sell goods worth over £16,000 to a customer and to accept for their payment two cheques which Gomez knew were stolen and worthless. Gomez assured his manager that he had found out about the cheques from the bank and the cheques were 'as good as cash'. The cheques were dishonoured on presentation. Gomez was later jointly charged with another for theft under s1(1) of the Theft Act 1968. He was convicted by the trial judge. The Court of Appeal, Criminal Division, allowed Gomez's appeal and quashed his conviction. The Crown's appeal to the House of Lords was on the ground that the Court of

Appeal was wrong in holding that there was no 'appropriation' within s1(1) of the Theft Act 1968. It would be too simplistic to look at the issues raised in *Gomez* as just one of statutory interpretation of ss 1 to 6 of the Theft Act 1968. The dichotomy between the majority – and that of the minority, as shown in the dissenting judgment of Lord Lowry, is both serious and fundamental. It relates to matters of *substance* as well as of *approach* in the interpretation of ss 1 to 6 of the Theft Act 1968.

To Lord Lowry, The Eighth Report of the Criminal Law Revision Committee, Theft and Related Offences is essential in construing the relevant provisions of the Theft Act 1968. But to Lord Keith, that report 'serves no useful purpose at the present time'.

Lord Lowry had no such inhibition as Lord Keith in using the Eighth Report, he said:

> 'Reading sections 1 to 6 as a whole, and also taking into account sections 24(4) and 28(6) the ordinary and natural meaning of "appropriation" in section 1(1) is confirmed. I would be very slow to concede that the word "appropriates" is in its context ambiguous.'

The net result of *Gomez* is that it is irrelevant for the purpose of theft that the act, with or without deception, was done with the authority or consent of the owner.

Extract adapted from 'To appropriate or not to appropriate, that is the question', Laurence Toczek *New Law Journal*, 15 December 2000

It is an unfortunate fact of life that the elderly and those with learning difficulties are particularly susceptible to having money extracted from them by the unscrupulous ... recent ... judgments ... make it clear that as well as being immoral, these activities may in certain circumstances be theft.

In *Williams* [the defendant] ran a building business. He was in the habit of charging elderly and vulnerable householders excessive amounts for building work. He was paid by means of bank and building society cheques. He was convicted of theft and the Court of Appeal rejected his appeal.

The main issue at the appeal was whether the defendant had appropriated property belonging to another. The prosecution's argument was: the appropriation was the act of presenting the cheques for payment; the property belonging to another was the

things in action belonging to the householders, namely that part of their bank or building society accounts which were extinguished when the cheques were honoured. ... [relying] on two cases *Kohn* and *Hallam*. The defence ... argued ... that the cases ... were no longer good law in the light of the House of Lords' decision in *Preddy* ... involving mortgage frauds.

The Court of Appeal rejected this argument [and] cited *Graham* '... theft of a chose in action may be committed when a chose in action belonging to another is destroyed by the defendant's act of appropriation ...'

In *Hinks* the defendant was a 'friend' of a man whose intellect was assessed by a consultant psychiatrist ... as between 70 and 80. The man had inherited approximately £60,000 from his father and had invested it in a building society. In the period April to November 1996, he withdrew most of the money and deposited it in an account belonging to the defendant ... on ... each occasion the man was accompanied by the defendant who did most of the talking ... The defendant was convicted of theft ... [when] her appeal failed ... the following question was certified for the House of Lords to consider:

'Whether the acquisition of an indefeasible title to property is capable of amounting to an appropriation ...'

The defence argued that *Gomez* was distinguishable as, in that case the deception practised on the manager rendered the transaction voidable. In the present case, however, whatever pressure the defendant exerted on the man was not sufficient to render the transaction void or voidable ... her actions were not 'unlawful' in the civil sense ... and the man could not have recovered in the civil courts.

Lord Steyn ... rejected the defence arguments [and said]:

> 'The purpose of the civil law and the criminal law are somewhat different. In a practical world there will sometimes be disharmony between [them]. ... The tension between [them] is ... not ... a factor which justifies a departure from the law as stated in *Lawrence* and *Gomez*.'

So cowboy builders and others who take advantage of the vulnerable for financial gain are guilty of theft (provided, of course, that the magistrates or jury conclude that they acted dishonestly).

8.3 Property

Extract from the Theft Act 1968 (s4)

4. 'Property'

(1) 'Property' includes money and all other property, real or personal, including things in action and other intangible property.

Extract adapted from the judgment in *Oxford v Moss* [1978] 68 Cr App R 183, QBD

Facts

An engineering student at Liverpool University stole the proof of an exam paper that he was due to sit the following month. The stipendiary magistrate (now District Judge Magistrates' Court) dismissed the case on the basis that the exam paper was not intangible property within the meaning of s4 of the Theft Act 1968. The prosecution appealed unsuccessfully by way of case stated.

Judgment

SMITH J:

By any standards, it was conduct which is to be condemned, and to the layman it would readily be described as cheating. The question raised is whether it is conduct which falls within the scope of the criminal law.

The question for this court is whether confidential information of this sort falls within that definition contained in s4(1). We have been referred to a number of authorities emanating from the area of trade secrets and matrimonial secrets.

Those are cases concerned with what is described as the duty to be of good faith. They are clear illustrations of the proposition that, if a person obtains information which is given to him in confidence and then sets out to take an unfair advantage of it, the courts will restrain him by way of an order of injunction or will condemn him in damages if an injunction is found to be inappropriate. It seems to me, speaking for my part, that they are of little assistance in the present situation in which we have to consider whether there is property in the information which is capable of being the subject of a charge of theft. In my judgment, it is clear that the answer to that question must be no.

8.4 Belonging to another

Extract from the Theft Act 1968 (s5)

5. 'Belonging to another'

(1) Property shall be regarded as belonging to any person having possession or control of it, or having in it any proprietary right or interest (not being an equitable interest arising only from an agreement to transfer or grant an interest).

(3) Where a person receives property from or on account of another, and is under an obligation to the other to retain and deal with that property or its proceeds in a particular way, the property or proceeds shall be regarded (as against him) as belonging to the other.

(4) Where a person gets property by another's mistake, and is under an obligation to make restoration (in whole or in part) of the property or its proceeds or of the value thereof, then to the extent of that obligation the property or proceeds shall be regarded (as against him) as belonging to the person entitled to restoration, and an intention not to make restoration shall be regarded accordingly as an intention to deprive that person of the property or proceeds.

Extract adapted from the judgment in *R v Woodman* [1974] QB 754

Facts

China Clays had run down its business and then sold the rights to all scrap metal on its site to another company. After that company had taken all of the metal that it wanted, China Clays then erected a fence around the site. There was still some scrap metal on the site and the defendant then came onto the site and removed it. The Court of Appeal, in upholding his conviction agreed that he had taken property belonging to another, even though China Clays no longer owned it.

Judgment

LORD WIDGERY CJ:

So far as this case is concerned, we are content to say that there was evidence that China Clays were in control of the site and *prima facie* in control of the articles on the site as well. The fact that it could not be shown that they were conscious of the existence of this or any particular scrap metal does not destroy the general principle that the control of a site by excluding others from it is *prima facie* control of articles on the site as well.

Extract adapted from the judgment in *R v Turner (No 2)* [1971] 1 WLR 901

Facts

Turner took his car to Brown's garage for repair. When it was ready he promised to return for the car and to pay the bill. Instead, he went that night with his spare keys and took the car. After the garage owner had located the car, Turner was convicted of its theft. He appealed unsuccessfully on the ground that within the meaning of s5 of the Theft Act 1968 it was not property 'belonging to another'.

Judgment

LORD PARKER CJ:

The words 'belonging to another' are specifically defined in section 5 of the Act: 'Property shall be regarded as belonging to any person having possession or control of it, or having in it any proprietary right or interest.' The sole question is whether Mr Brown had possession or control.

This court is satisfied that there is no ground whatever for qualifying the words 'possession or control' in any way. It is sufficient if it is found that the person from whom the property is taken, or to use the words of the Act, appropriated, was at the time in fact in possession or control. At the trial there was a long argument as to whether that possession or control must be lawful, it

being said that by reason of the fact that this car was subject to a hire-purchase agreement, Mr Brown could never even as against the defendant obtain lawful possession or control. As I have said, this court is quite satisfied that the judge was quite correct in telling the jury they need not bother about lien, and that they need not bother about hire-purchase agreements. The only question was whether Mr Brown was in fact in possession of control.

Extract adapted from the judgment in *R v Hall* [1973] 1 QB 126

Facts

Hall was a travel agent. He received money from clients as deposits for holidays. This money was put into the firm's general account. When certain holidays were not forthcoming, not only were the clients deeply upset but Hall was also convicted of theft of the money. He successfully appealed on the ground that, under s5(3) of the Theft Act 1968, he had not been placed under any obligation to retain or deal with the money in any particular way.

Judgment

EDMUND DAVIES LJ:

Point (1) turns on the application of section 5(3) of the Theft Act 1968, which provides: 'Where a person receives property from or on account of another, and is under an obligation to the other to retain and deal with that property or its proceeds in a particular way, the property or proceeds shall be regarded (as against him) as belonging to the other.'

Counsel for the appellant submitted that in the circumstances arising in these seven cases there arose no such 'obligation' on the appellant. He referred us to the Eighth Report of the Criminal Law Revision Committee: 'Subsection (3) provides for the special case where property is transferred to a person to retain and deal with for a particular purpose and he misapplies it or its proceeds. An example would be the treasurer of a holiday fund. The person in question is in law the owner of the property; but the subsection treats the property, as against him, as belonging to the persons to whom he owes the duty to retain and deal with the property as agreed. He will therefore be guilty of stealing from them if he misapplies the property or its proceeds.' What counsel for the appellant resists is that in such circumstances the travel agent 'is under an obligation' to the client 'to retain and deal with ... in a particular way' sums paid to him in such circumstances.

Nevertheless, when a client goes to a firm carrying on the business of travel agents and pays them money, he expects that in return he will, in due course, receive the tickets and other documents necessary for him to accomplish the trip which he is paying for, and the firm are 'under an obligation' to perform their part to fulfil his expectation and are liable to pay him damages if they do not. But, in our judgment, what was not here established was that these clients expected him to 'retain and deal with that property or its proceeds in a particular way,' and that an 'obligation' to do so was undertaken by the appellant. We must make clear, however, that each case turns on its own facts. Cases could, we suppose, conceivably arise where by some special arrangement, the client could impose on the travel agent an 'obligation' falling within section 5(3). But no such special arrangement was made in any of the seven cases here being considered.

It follows from this that, despite what on any view must be condemned as scandalous conduct by the appellant, in our judgment on this ground alone this appeal must be allowed and the conviction quashed.

Extract adapted from the judgment in *R v Gilks* [1971] 1 WLR 1341, CA

Facts

A betting shop clerk mistakenly paid Gilks's winnings on a horse that had in fact lost. Gilks realised the mistake but kept the money anyway. He was convicted of theft and appealed unsuccessfully. The court considered also s5(4) of the Theft Act 1968 which the court had said had no application to the case or if it did then s5(4) included an obligation which was not a legal obligation. Gilks had appealed that these directions to the jury were wrong.

Judgment

CAIRNS LJ:
The gap in the law which section 5(4) of the Theft Act 1968 was designed to fill was, as the deputy chairman rightly held, that which is illustrated by *Moynes v Cooper*. There a workman received a pay packet containing £7 more than was due to him but did not become aware of the overpayment until he opened the envelope some time later. He then kept the £7. This was held not to be theft because there was no *animus furandi* at the moment of taking. It would be strange indeed if section 5(4) of the Theft Act 1968, which was designed to bring within the net of theft a type of dishonest behaviour which escaped before, were to be held to have created a loophole for another type of dishonest behaviour which was always within the net.

An alternative ground on which the deputy chairman held that the money should be regarded as belonging to Ladbrokes was that 'obligation' in section 5(4) meant an obligation whether a legal one or not. In the opinion of this court that was an incorrect ruling. In a

criminal statute, where a person's criminal liability is made dependent on his having an obligation, it would be quite wrong to construe that word so as to cover a moral or social obligation as distinct from a legal one.

Read the five extracts above and answer the questions

Questions:

1. How does the scrap metal in *Woodman* fit into the definition of 'belonging to another' in s5(1) of the Theft Act 1968?
2. How could Turner steal his own car?
3. Why was it impossible to convict Hall under the meaning of s5(3) despite the fact that his behaviour was described as 'scandalous'?
4. Why is a defendant guilty of theft under s5(4) when (s)he has only come by the property by mistake?

Try this sample A Level exam problem:

Suggest whether there is 'property belonging to another' sufficient for a conviction of theft in the following situations:

(a) My flatmate gives me money to pay the gas bill. I spend it on some law books.
(b) By mistake, Hodder give me two cheques for royalties. I refuse to return one.
(c) I take a law book belonging to the college library from the house of a student who has had it for some years but I do not take it back to the library.

8.5 Intention permanently to deprive

Extract from the Theft Act 1968 (s6)

6. **'With the intention of permanently depriving the other of it'**

(1) A person appropriating property belonging to another without meaning the other permanently to lose the thing itself is nevertheless to be regarded as having the intention of permanently depriving the other of it if his intention is to treat the thing as his own to dispose of regardless of the other's rights; and a borrowing or lending of it may amount to so treating it if, but only if, the borrowing or lending is for a period and in

circumstances making it equivalent to an outright taking or disposal.

Extract adapted from the judgment in *R v Lloyd and Others* [1985] QB 829, CA

Facts

Lloyd was a projectionist at a cinema. With two others he arranged to take films in order to copy them and then to put them back. They were convicted of a conspiracy to steal but on appeal the convictions were quashed since no intention to permanently deprive could be shown.

Judgment

LORD LANE CJ:
We turn now to the provisions of the Theft Act ... On that wording alone these appellants were not guilty of theft or conspiracy to steal. The success of their scheme and their ability to act with impunity in a similar fashion in the future, depended on their ability to return the film to its rightful place in the hands of the Odeon cinema at Barking as rapidly as possibly, so that its absence should not be noticed. Therefore the intention of the appellants could more accurately be described as an intention temporarily to deprive the owner of the film and was indeed the opposite of an intention to permanently deprive.

It seems to us that in this case we are concerned with the second part of s6(1), namely the words after the semi-colon.

These films, it could be said, were borrowed by Lloyd from his employers in order to enable him and the others to carry out their 'piracy' exercise.

Borrowing is *ex hypothesi* not something which is done with an intention to permanently deprive. This half of the subsection, we believe, is intended to make it clear that a mere borrowing is never enough to constitute the necessary guilty mind unless the intention is to return the 'thing' in such a changed state that it can truly be said that all its goodness or virtue has gone.

That being the case, we turn to inquire whether the feature films in this case fall within this category. Our view is that they cannot.

Answer the two extracts above and answer the questions

Questions:

1. Why could it not be proved that the projectionist in *Lloyd* intended to permanently deprive the cinema of the film?
2. If my son borrowed my Wolverhampton Wanderers FC season ticket ten matches before the end of the season, went to the matches, and then gave me the season ticket book back after the final game, would he be guilty of theft, and, if so, why?

Revision exercise:
TRUE OR FALSE: on Theft

Below are 10 statements about the offence of theft. In the column on the right, identify whether the statement is true or false.

1	The *mens rea* for theft is dishonesty	
2	You could be convicted of stealing your own property	
3	Wild flowers can never be stolen	
4	If I used my friend's season ticket to get into the Wolves football matches while he thought that it was lost, I would not be stealing	
5	It is not dishonest if you borrow your friend's goods, thinking that he will let you borrow them	
6	If I am overpaid wages by my employer's mistake, I do not have to return the money	
7	A wild animal could never be stolen	
8	If my flatmate gave me her half of the rent to pay to the landlord I could be guilty of theft if I spent it and then did not pay the rent	
9	I am not guilty of theft if I take something I want and leave enough money to pay for it	
10	I can never be guilty of theft if I have the owner's permission to take his property	

Guess the case!

Fig 8.1

A robbery is a theft accompanied by some force. Problems usually concern what level of force must be applied and also the point at which the force is appropriate.

Extract from the Theft Act 1968 (s8)

8. Robbery

(1) A person is guilty of robbery if he steals, and immediately before or at the time of doing so, and in order to do so, he uses force on any person or puts or seeks to put any person in fear of being then and there subjected to force.

Extract adapted from the judgment in *Dawson* [1976] 64 Cr App R 170

Facts

Three men jostled a sailor and while he was struggling to keep his balance one of the three was able to steal the sailor's wallet. They were convicted of robbery and appealed unsuccessfully on the issue of whether their actions could amount to 'force'.

Judgment

LAWTON LJ:
Mr Locke had submitted at the end of the prosecution's case that what had happened could not in law amount to the use of force. He called the learned judge's attention to some old authorities and ... submitted that because of those old authorities there was not enough evidence to go to the jury.

The object of the Act was to get rid of all the old technicalities of the law of larceny and to put the law into simple language which juries would understand and which they themselves would use. That is what has happened in section 8 which defines 'robbery'.

The choice of the word 'force' is not without interest because under the Larceny Act 1916 the word 'violence' had been used, but Parliament deliberately on the advice of the Criminal Law Revision Committee changed that word to 'force'. Whether there is any difference between 'violence' or 'force' is not relevant for the purposes of this case; but the word is 'force'. It

is a word in ordinary use. It is a word which juries understand. The learned judge left it to say whether jostling a man in the way which the victim described to such an extent that he had difficulty in keeping his balance could be said to be the use of force. The learned judge, because of the argument put forward by Mr Locke, went out of his way to explain to the jury that force in these sort of circumstances must be substantial to justify a verdict.

Whether it was right for him to put that adjective before the word 'force' when Parliament had not done so we will not discuss for the purposes of this case. It was a matter for the jury. They were there to use their common sense and knowledge of the world. We cannot say that their decision as to whether force was used was wrong. They were entitled to the view that force was used.

Extract adapted from the judgment in *Hale* [1978] 68 Cr App R 415

Facts

Two men entered the victim's house wearing stockings over their faces as masks. Hale put his hand over the victim's mouth to stop her screaming while the other man went upstairs and took jewellery. They then tied her up and threatened that they would harm her child if she phoned the police within five minutes of them leaving. Hale was convicted of robbery and appealed unsuccessfully on the basis that any force used did not come before or at the time of the theft.

Judgment

EVELEIGH LJ:
In so far as the facts of the present case are concerned, counsel submitted that the theft was completed when the jewellery box was first seized and any force thereafter could not have been 'immediately before or at the time of stealing' and certainly not 'in order to steal'. The essence of the submission was that the theft was completed as soon as the jewellery box was seized.

Section 8 of the Theft Act begins: 'A person is guilty of robbery if he steals ...' He steals when he acts in accordance with the basic definition of theft in section 1 of the Theft Act; that is to say when he dishonestly appropriates property belonging to another with an intention of permanently depriving the other of it. It thus becomes necessary to consider what is 'appropriation' or, according to section 3, 'any assumption by a person of the rights of an owner'. An assumption of rights ... is conduct which usurps the rights of the owner. To say that the conduct is over and done with as soon as he lays hands on the property, or when he first manifests an intention to deal with it as his own, is contrary to common-sense and to the natural meaning of the words.

In the present case there can be little doubt that if the appellant had been interrupted after the seizure of the jewellery box the jury would have been entitled to find that the appellant and his accomplice were assuming the rights of an owner at the time when the jewellery box was seized. However, the act of appropriation does not suddenly cease. It is a continuous act and it is a matter for the jury to decide whether or not the act of appropriation has finished. Moreover, it is quite clear that the intention to deprive the owner permanently, which accompanied the assumption of the owner's rights, was a continuing one at all material times. This Court therefore rejects the contention that the theft had ceased by the time the lady was tied up. As a matter of common-sense the appellant was in the course of committing the theft; he was stealing.

There remains the question whether there was robbery. Quite clearly the jury were at liberty to find the appellant guilty of robbery relying upon the force used when he put his hand over Mrs Carrett's mouth to restrain her from calling for help. We also think that they were also entitled to rely upon the act of tying her up provided they were satisfied (and it is difficult to see how they could not be satisfied) that the force so used was to enable them to steal.

Extract adapted from the judgment in *Corcoran v Anderton* [1980] 71 Cr App R 104

Facts

The defendants had accosted their victim with a view to snatching her handbag. One struck her in the back from behind and a struggle ensued for control of the handbag. The struggle caused the victim to release the bag which then fell to the floor, but the man ran away to avoid capture. His accomplice was convicted of robbery. In his cases stated appeal he argued that there could be no robbery since control of the bag was never gained at any time, so that there was no appropriation. His appeal failed.

Judgment

WATKINS J:

So confining myself to the facts as found by the justices in the instant case, I think that an 'appropriation' takes place when an accused snatches a woman's handbag completely from her grasp, so that she no longer has physical control of it because it has fallen to the ground. What has been involved in such activity as that, bearing in mind the dishonest state of mind of the accused, is an assumption of the rights of the owner, a taking of the property of another. If one had to consider the definition of 'theft' as contained in the Larceny Act 1916, it is inevitable, so it seems to me, that there was here a sufficient taking and carrying away to satisfy the definition of 'theft' in that Act. In my judgment there cannot possibly be, save for the instance where a handbag is carried away from the scene of it, a clearer instance of robbery than that which these justices found was committed.

Turning to the actual question posed to this Court. 'Could the tugging at the handbag, accompanied by force, amount to robbery, notwithstanding that the co-accused did not have sole control of the bag at any time?' in my opinion, which may be contrary to some notions of what constitutes a sufficient appropriation to satisfy the definition of that word in section 3(1) of the Theft Act, the forcible tugging of the handbag of itself could in the circumstances be a sufficient exercise of control by the accused person so as to amount to an assumption by him of the rights of the owner, and therefore an appropriation of the property.

Read the four extracts above and answer the questions

Questions:

1. What particular feature distinguishes a robbery from any other theft?
2. In *Dawson*, what definition of the word 'force' does Lord Justice Lawton give?
3. In the light of the result of the case, what difference do you think there is between the words 'force' and 'violence'?
4. What degree of 'force' is sufficient, according to the judgment in *Hale*?
5. What difficulty is presented in the case of *Hale* and how did Lord Justice Eveleigh see this being overcome?
6. Based on the extracts, does an accused actually have to get away with the property?
7. What argument was put by the appellant in *Corcoran v Anderton* and why did the argument fail?

Answer the clues 1–7 in the spaces in the crossword below to discover an important case to the development of robbery in the shaded line reading across.

CLUES
1. May the .... be with you. If it's not then there is no robbery.
2. What you are actually hoping to do at the time of the robbery?
3. Would his victim have challenged him to a duel involving handbags at dawn?
4. And where the handbag fell in the case.
5. This defendant did more than say 'Hello sailor'!
6. So what act is robbery a part of?
7. Though it might have been necessary before 1968 it may not be now!

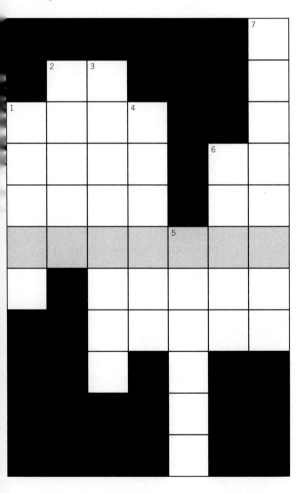

CHAPTER 10

PROPERTY OFFENCES: BURGLARY

There are two separate offences of burglary, both of which involve trespassing onto premises. One set of offences involves entering with intent to commit one of four further offences. The other type involves one of two offences being carried out after the entry. The obvious question is whether the law needs to be so complex. Problems in the past have concerned the trespass and what it will

Extract from the Theft Act 1968 (s9)

9. Burglary

(1) A person is guilty of burglary if –
   (a) he enters any building or part of a building as a trespasser and with intent to commit any such offence as is mentioned in subsection (2) below; or
   (b) having entered any building or part of a building as a trespasser he steals or attempts to steal anything in the building or that part of it or inflicts or attempts to inflict on any person therein any grievous bodily harm.

(2) The offences referred to in subsection (1)(a) above are offences of stealing anything in the building or part of a building in question, of inflicting on any person therein any grievous bodily harm or raping any person therein, and of doing unlawful damage to the building or anything therein.

(4) References in subsections (1) and (2) above to a building, and the references in subsection (3) above to a building which is a dwelling, shall apply also to an inhabited vehicle or vessel, and shall apply to any such vehicle or vessel at times when the person having a habitation in it is not there as well as at times when he is.

Extract adapted from the judgment in *R v Collins* [1973] 1 QB 100, CA

Collins was convicted of burglary with intent to rape under s9(1)(a) Theft Act 1968. He appealed successfully. The facts are dealt with in detail in the judgment of Lord Justice Edmund Davies below.

Judgment

EDMUND DAVIES LJ:
Let me relate the facts. Were they put into a novel or portrayed on the stage, they would be regarded as being so improbable as to be unworthy of serious consideration and as at times verging on farce. At about 2 o'clock in the early morning … a young lady of 18 went to bed at her mother's home … She had taken a certain amount of drink …

She has the habit of sleeping without wearing night apparel in a bed which is very near the lattice type window of her room.

At about 3.30 she awoke and she then saw in the moonlight a vague form crouched in the open window. She was unable to remember, and this is important, whether the form was on the outside of the window sill or on that part of the sill which was inside the room, and for reasons which will later become clear, that seemingly narrow point is of crucial importance.

The young lady then realised several things: first of all that the form in the window was that of a male; secondly that he was a naked male; and thirdly, that he was a naked male with an erect penis. She also saw in the moonlight that his hair was blonde. She thereupon leapt to the conclusion that her boyfriend, with whom for some time she had been on terms of regular and frequent sexual intimacy, was paying her an ardent nocturnal visit. She promptly sat up in bed, and the man descended from the sill and joined her in bed and they had full sexual intercourse. But there was something about him that made her think that things were not as they usually were between her and her boyfriend. So she turned on the bed-side light, saw that her companion was not her boyfriend and slapped the face of the intruder. He said to her, 'Give me a good time tonight,' and got hold of her arm, but she bit him and told him to go … he promptly vanished.

The complainant said that she would not have agreed to intercourse if she had known that the person entering her room was not her boyfriend. But there was no suggestion of any force having being used upon her, and the intercourse which took place was undoubtedly effected with no resistance on her part.

The defendant was seen by the police [and] the conversation which took place elicited these points: He was very lustful the previous night. He had taken a lot of drink ... he knew the complainant because he had worked around her house. On this occasion, desiring sexual intercourse ... he walked around the house, saw a light in an upstairs bedroom, and he knew that this was the girl's bedroom. He found a step ladder, leaned it against the wall and climbed up and looked into the bedroom. He could see through the wide-open window a girl who was naked and asleep. So he descended the ladder and stripped off all his clothes, with the exception of his socks, because apparently he took the view that if the girl's mother entered the bedroom it would be easier to effect a rapid escape if he had his socks on than if he was in his bare feet.

Having undressed, he then climbed the ladder and pulled himself up on to the window sill. His version of the matter is that he was pulling himself in when she awoke. She then got up and knelt on the bed, she put her arms around his neck and body, and she seemed to pull him into the bed.

Now one feature of the case which remained at the conclusion of the evidence in great obscurity is where exactly Collins was at the moment when, according to him, the girl manifested that she was welcoming him. Was he kneeling on the sill outside the window or was he already in the room, having climbed through the window frame, and kneeling upon the inner sill? It was a crucial matter, for there were certainly three ingredients that it was incumbent upon the Crown to establish. Under s9 of the Theft Act 1968 ... the entry of the accused into the building must first be proved. Secondly, it must be proved that he entered as a trespasser. Thirdly, it must be proved that he entered as a trespasser with intent at the time of entry to commit rape therein.

The second ingredient of the offence – the entry must be as a trespasser – is one which has not, to the best of our knowledge been previously canvassed in the courts.

What does that involve? According to the editors of *Archibold Criminal Pleading* 'Any intentional, reckless or negligent entry into a building will, it would appear, constitute a trespass if the building is in the possession of another person who does not consent to the entry'.

A view contrary to that ... was expressed by Professor Smith's book on *The Law of Theft* 'D should be acquitted on the ground of lack of *mens rea*. Though, under the civil law, he entered as a trespasser, it is submitted that he cannot be convicted of the criminal offence unless he knew of the facts which caused him to be a trespasser or, at least, was reckless.'

The matter has also been dealt with by Professor Griew ... 'What if D wrongly believes that he is not trespassing ... for the purpose of criminal liability a man should be judged on the basis of the facts as he believed them to be ... D should be liable for burglary only if he knowingly trespasses or is reckless as to whether he trespasses or not'.

We prefer the view expressed by Professor Smith and Professor Griew ... there cannot be a conviction for entering premises 'as a trespasser' within the meaning of section 9 of the Theft Act unless the person entering does so knowing that he is a trespasser and nevertheless deliberately enters, or, at the very least, is reckless as to whether or not he is entering the premises of another without the other party's consent.

Having so held, the pivotal point of this appeal is whether the Crown established that this defendant at the moment he entered the bedroom knew perfectly well that he was not welcome there, or being reckless as to whether he was welcome or not, was nevertheless determined to enter. That in turn involves consideration as to where he was at the time the complainant indicated that she was welcoming him into the bedroom.

Unless the jury were entirely satisfied that the defendant made an effective and substantial entry into the bedroom without the complainant doing or saying anything to cause him to believe that she was consenting to his entering it, he ought not to be convicted of the offence charged.

We have to say that this appeal must be allowed on the basis that the jury were never invited to consider the vital question whether this young man did enter the premises as a trespasser.

Extract adapted from the judgment in *R v Walkington* [1979] 1 WLR 1169

Facts

The defendant was seen loitering near tills in Debenhams in Oxford Street while cashing up was in process. He then went into a till area, which was for staff only, and which was unattended. He looked into the partly open cash drawer and then slammed it shut when he saw that it was empty. He was convicted of burglary with intent to steal, contrary to s9(1)(a) Theft Act 1968, and appealed unsuccessfully.

Judgment

GEOFFREY LANE LJ:

It seems to this court that in the end one simply has to go back to the words of the Act itself and if the jury are satisfied so as to feel sure that the defendant had entered any building or part of a building as a trespasser, and are satisfied that at the moment of entering he intended to steal anything in the building or that part of the building, the fact that there was nothing in the building worth while to steal seems to us to be immaterial. He nevertheless had the intent to steal. As we see, to hold otherwise would be to make a nonsense of this part of the Act and cannot have been the intention of the legislature at the time when the Theft Act 1968 was passed. Nearly every prospective burglar could no doubt truthfully say that he only intended to steal if he found something in the building worth stealing.

Read the three extracts above and answer the questions

Questions:

1. How many different offences of burglary are there?
2. What are the basic differences between s9(1)(a) and s9(1)(b)?
3. According to Lord Justice Edmund Davies in *Collins*, what are the necessary features of a trespass in order for there to be a burglary?
4. Why was Collins not a burglar?
5. What effect does the defendant's state of mind have on the trespass?
6. What does the case of *Walkington* reveal about the meaning of 'part of a building'?
7. How broad is the definition of 'building' in the Act?

Revision Exercise:
QUICK QUIZ: BURGLARY PROBLEMS

Consider which of the following could involve a burglary and suggest whether this would be under s9(1)(a) or s9(1)(b):

1. Jerry, a known drug abuser, is found at 2 o'clock in the morning having broken into a chemist's shop. He has no drugs on him.
2. Jerry is caught with his arm reaching inside a jeweller's window, with his hand full of rings, having been seen smashing the window first with a brick.
3. Jerry, a known drug abuser, is found by police in the back yard of a chemist's shop after closing hours.
4. Jerry has been caught by store detectives in a store room, access to which is prohibited to the public.
5. Jerry stole a tray of apple pies which were resting on Mavis's window sill, cooling.
6. Jerry and his friend Terry are discovered coming out of Jerry's father's house and handing over Jerry's father's television set to their drug dealer in return for drugs.
7. Jerry is caught breaking in to a house boat on the river. The owner normally lives there but is away on holiday.

CHAPTER 11

PROPERTY OFFENCES: DECEPTION OFFENCES

Deception offences have caused many problems of interpretation and led to further enactment and there are a great number of different offences. There is a confusing overlap between theft under s1 and obtaining property by deception under s15.

Obtaining property by deception

Extract from the Theft Act 1968 (s15(4))

(4) For purposes of this section 'deception' means any deception (whether deliberate or reckless) by words or conduct as to fact or as to law, including a deception as to the present intentions of the party using the deception or any other person.

Extract from the Theft Act 1968 (s15(1))

15. Obtaining property by deception

(1) A person who by any deception dishonestly obtains property belonging to another, with the intention of permanently depriving the other of it, shall on conviction on indictment be liable to imprisonment for a period not exceeding ten years.

Extract adapted from the judgment in *R v Charles* [1977] AC 171, HL

Facts

Charles had a bank account and was given a cheque book and a cheque guarantee card with a limit of £30 per cheque. The bank manager had previously told him that he was not to use the cheque card more than once in a day. Charles used a complete book of 25 cheques, written for £30 each, to buy chips at a gambling club, knowing that he had insufficient funds in the bank but that it would honour each cheque because it was within the limit of the cheque guarantee card. He was convicted of deception and his appeal in the House of Lords failed.

Judgment

LORD DIPLOCK:

The whole foundation of liability under the doctrine of ostensible authority is a representation, believed by the person to whom it is made, that the person claiming to contract as agent for a principal has the actual authority of the principal to enter the contract on his behalf.

That is the representation that the drawer makes to the payee when he uses a cheque card to back a cheque which he draws in compliance with the conditions endorsed on the card. That in the instant case Mr Cersell, the manager of the gaming club, so understood it is implicit from the passage in his evidence to which my noble and learned friend, Lord Edmund Davies, refers. Mr Cersell may not have known the doctrine of ostensible authority under that name, but he knew what it was all about. He would not have taken the accused's cheques had he not believed that the accused was authorised by the bank to use the cheque card to back them.

Read the three extracts above and answer the questions

Questions:

1. What is a deception, according to the sources?
2. In what circumstances might a deception 'by conduct' occur?
3. What similarities are there between s15 and s1 Theft Act 1968?
4. What was the deception in *Charles*?
5. Give an example of deception as to law.
6. Give an example of deception as to fact.
7. Give an example of deception as to the present intentions of the party making the deception.

11.2 Obtaining services by deception

Extract from the Theft Act 1978 (s1(1) and s1(2))

1. Obtaining services by deception

(1) A person who by any deception dishonestly obtains services from another shall be guilty of an offence.

(2) It is an obtaining of services where the other is induced to confer a benefit by doing some act, or causing or permitting some act to be done, on the understanding that the benefit has been or will be paid for.

Questions:

1. What is the crucial feature about the service for a successful charge of s1?
2. What differences between s1 of the 1978 Act and s15 of the 1968 Act are apparent?

11.3 Evasion of liability

Extract from the Theft Act 1978 (s2(1))

2. Evasion of liability by deception

(1) Subject to subsection (2) below, where a person by any deception–
  (a) dishonestly secures the remission of the whole or part of any existing liability to make a payment, whether his own liability or another's; or
  (b) with intent to make permanent default in whole or in part on any existing liability to make a payment, or with intent to let another do so, dishonestly indices the creditor or any person claiming payment on behalf of the creditor to wait for payment (whether or not the due date for payment is deferred) or to forego payment; or
  (c) dishonestly obtains any exemption from or abatement of liability to make a payment;
he shall be guilty of an offence.

Extract adapted from the judgment in *R v Firth* (1990) 91 Cr App Rep 217, CA

Facts

The defendant, a consultant gynaecologist, had some of his private patients admitted to an NHS hospital without informing the hospital that they were private patients, so that neither he nor the patients, were charged for their treatment. He appealed unsuccessfully against his conviction under s2(1)(c) for evading liability by deception.

Judgment

LORD LANE CJ:
If, as was alleged, it was incumbent upon him to give the information to the hospital and he deliberately and dishonestly refrained from doing so, with the result that no charge was levied either upon the patients or upon himself, in our judgment the wording and subsection which I have just read is satisfied. It matters not whether it was an act of commission or an act of omission. Provided those matters were substantiated the prosecution had made out their case.

Read the two extracts above and answer the questions

Questions:

1. What feature is common to s2(1)(a) and (b) but not a feature of (c)?
2. What is the basic difference between s2(1)(a) and (b)?
3. Why should Lord Lane say that it is unimportant whether it is an act or an omission in *Firth*?

11.4 Making off without payment

Extract from the Theft Act 1978 (s3(1))

3. Making off without payment

(1) Subject to subsection (3) below, a person who, knowing payment on the spot for any goods supplied or service done is required or expected from him, dishonestly makes off without having paid as required or expected and with intent to avoid payment of the amount due shall be guilty of an offence.

Extract from 'Case and Comment. Theft Act 1978, s3 – making off without payment from the "spot" *R v Aziz*, *Criminal Law Review*, September 1993, p 708 (Commentary by Professor Sir John Smith)

Facts

D and B requested a taxi [and] on arrival they refused to pay the fare ... The driver ... decided to take them to the police station. B ... tried to put the gear lever into reverse ... and [D and B] both ran away. The taxi driver ran after them and caught D [who was convicted] of making off without payment ... On appeal it was contended that the direction to the jury was inadequate [they] should have been directed to consider whether the requirement for payment had ceased because the taxi driver had announced his intention to take the passengers back to the hotel ...

Held

... the Act did not require payment to be made at any particular spot. The words 'on the spot' – or 'there and then' as the Criminal Law Revision Committee paraphrased them related to the knowledge which the customer had to have of when payment was to be made. The words 'dishonestly makes off without payment' were not qualified in any way ... The words 'makes off' involved a departure without paying from the place where payment would normally be made. In this case, payment was requested whilst the fares were still in the cab. The fact that [the driver] drove off to the police station or somewhere else, locking the door, did not mean that when D ran off he could not be making off without having paid, dishonestly intending to avoid payment. It was the time at which he made off which was critical at which he had to have formed the intent to avoid payment.

Commentary

In the usual type of case the 'spot' on which payment is required or expected is the spot from which the defendant is alleged to have made off, but the Act does not in terms require that it should be so.

In the present case the nightclub was the spot where payment was required or expected but the driver continued to require and expect payment from D as he drove him away, whether to the hotel or to the police station, and D could hardly have supposed otherwise. The requirement and expectation of the fare ... was continuing throughout the journey, so that the spot was in motion. If that is right, making off at any point constituted the offence.

Read the two extracts above and answer the questions

Questions:

1. What is important about the defendant's state of mind for s3?
2. What does the case of *Aziz* and Professor Smith's commentary tell us about the meaning of 'the spot where payment is required'?

Revision exercise:
QUICK QUIZ: DECEPTION PROBLEMS

Try to decide which deception or other offence from this chapter is a possible charge in the following examples. Identify it by section number and 1968 or 1978 Act in the right-hand column

1	Kevin gets on a bus to go to work and flashes an out-of-date student pass at the driver, hoping that the driver will not notice	
2	Kelly goes into a café and picks up money on a table left as a tip and uses it to buy a coffee	
3	Kieran tells his landlord that he has no money and asks if he will wait until next Friday when Kieran will pay him two weeks' rent. Kieran then leaves secretly during the night	
4	Khan goes to Bingo and pays for a book of Bingo cards with her credit card, knowing that she has already exceeded her credit limit	
5	Kermit has just eaten at his local curry house and, while the waiter has gone back out into the kitchen to bring him the bill, he has left the restaurant	

Guess the case!

Fig 11.1

CHAPTER 12

PROPERTY OFFENCES: CRIMINAL DAMAGE

Criminal damage offences like theft are offences against property. They differ because they involve damage or destruction rather than an interference with rights of ownership. They can be very serious if the damage is caused by fire (arson) or if done with the purpose of endangering life or reckless as to that possibility.

Extract from the Criminal Damage Act 1971 (s1)

1. Destroying or damaging property

(1) A person who without lawful excuse destroys or damages any property belonging to another intending to destroy or damage any such property or being reckless as to whether any such property would be destroyed or damaged shall be guilty of an offence.

(2) A person who without lawful excuse destroys or damages any property, whether belonging to himself or another–

    (a)   intending to destroy or damage any property or being reckless as to whether any property would be destroyed or damaged; and

    (b)   intending by the destruction or damage to endanger the life of another or being reckless as to whether the life of another would be thereby endangered;

shall be guilty of an offence.

(3) An offence committed under this section by destroying or damaging property by fire shall be charged as arson.

Extract adapted from the judgment in *Caldwell* [1981] 1 All ER 961

Facts

Caldwell felt he had a legitimate grievance against a hotel owner and set fire to the hotel. Although 10 guests were staying in the hotel at the time of the fire, it was quickly put out without serious damage. Caldwell was convicted of arson and recklessly endangering life under the Criminal Damage Act 1971 and failed in his appeal also.

Judgment

LORD DIPLOCK:

As respects the charge under section 1(2) the prosecution did not rely upon an actual intent ... to endanger the lives of the residents but relied upon his having been reckless whether the lives of any of them would be endangered. His act of setting fire to it was one which the jury were entitled to think created an obvious risk that the lives of the residents would be endangered; and the only defence ... is that the respondent had made himself so drunk as to render him oblivious of that risk.

If the only mental state capable of constituting the necessary *mens rea* for an offence under section 1(2) were ... 'intending by the destruction or damage to endanger the life of another,' it would have been necessary to consider whether the offence was to be classified as one of 'specific' intent for the purpose of the rule of law which this House affirmed and applied in *R v Majewski*, and this it plainly is. But this is not ... a relevant enquiry where 'being reckless as to whether the life of another would be thereby endangered' is an alternative mental state that is capable of constituting the necessary *mens rea* of the offence with which he is charged.

Reducing oneself by drink or drugs to a condition in which the restraints of reason and conscience are cast off was held to be a reckless course of conduct and an integral part of the crime.

So [here], the fact that the respondent was unaware of the risk of endangering the lives of the residents in the hotel owing to his self-induced intoxication, would be no defence if ... obvious to him had he been sober.

Extract adapted from the judgment in *Elliott v C (a Minor)* [1983] 77 Cr App R 103

Facts

A 14-year-old girl of low intelligence stayed out all night without sleep in a garden shed. She poured white spirit onto carpet in the shed and lit it to keep warm. The shed was destroyed and she was charged under the Criminal Damage Act 1971. Magistrates acquitted her because her age, low intelligence and lack of sleep meant there was no obvious risk of damage. The prosecution appealed by way of case stated and the divisional court, applying *Caldwell*, felt compelled to allow the appeal.

Judgment

ROBERT GOFF LJ:

I agree with ... Glidewell J but ... simply because I believe myself constrained to do so by authority.

This is not a case where there was a deliberate disregard of a known risk of damage or injury ...; nor ... where there was a mindless indifference to a risk of such damage or injury; nor ... where failure to give thought to the ... risk was due to some blameworthy cause such as intoxication.

Where a judge [must] reach a conclusion he senses to be unjust or inappropriate, he [has] a duty to examine the precedent with scrupulous care to ascertain whether he can ... legitimately interpret or qualify the principle ... to achieve the result which [is] just or appropriate in the particular case.

Read the three extracts above and answer the questions

Questions:

1. What is the necessary mental intent for criminal damage under s1(1) of the Act?
2. What are the essential differences in the offence under s1(2)?
3. Why do you think that there is a separate offence of arson?
4. How was the mental element in *Caldwell* described?
5. Why was the defendant's drunken state no defence in the case?
6. Why does Goff LJ think it is unfair to have to apply the *ratio* of *Caldwell* in *Elliott v C*?
7. What does this say about objective recklessness?

Revision exercise:
QUICK QUIZ: CRIMINAL DAMAGE PROBLEMS

Consider which of the following could involve criminal damage under s1(1), s1(2), or s1(3) of the 1971 Act

1. A 15-year-old boy has thrown down a lighted firework in a shop and this has caused a fire destroying the shop
2. A drunk spits on my new suit as I pass him in the street
3. An animal rights activist paints slogans on the wall of a laboratory carrying out tests on animals
4. I hire scaffolding to paint my house and carelessly scratch one pole when I let it fall while assembling it
5. A man who is upset by the loud music played constantly by his neighbours throws a lighted petrol bomb against their outside wall. The petrol bomb destroys a bush and burns itself out

There are a variety of defences to crimes. Some such as insanity operate because they prevent the defendant from forming the necessary intent. Some, like automatism, operate because they also mean that conduct is involuntary so the *actus reus* is not made out either. Intoxication on the other hand if it is self-induced begins with voluntary actions so that the defence is harder to use.

Infancy and lack of capacity

Extract from the Children and Young Persons Act 1933 (s50)

50. Age of criminal responsibility

It shall be conclusively presumed that no child under the age of ten years can be guilty of any offence.

Extract adapted from the judgment in *C v DPP* [1995] 2 All ER 43, HL

Facts

A 12-year-old boy was convicted by magistrates of interfering with a motor vehicle with intent to commit a theft, contrary to s9(1) Criminal Attempts Act 1981, after being caught tampering with a motor cycle and then running away. He appealed by way of case stated on the presumption of *doli incapax*, i.e. that a child aged between 10 and 14, who was charged with a criminal offence, was presumed not to know that his act was seriously wrong unless the prosecution could prove that in fact the child knew that what he did was seriously wrong. The Divisional Court upheld the conviction holding that the presumption was outdated. He then appealed to the House of Lords on the basis that the Divisional Court had indulged in 'unjustified law making'.

Judgment

LORD LOWRY:
... the imperfections that have been attributed to [the presumption] cannot, in my view, provide a justification for saying that [it] is no longer part of our law. To sweep it away under the doubtful auspices of judicial legislation is to my mind, quite impracticable.

Clearly then ... the presumption, for better or worse, applies to cases like the present ... what must be proved in order to rebut the presumption...

A long and uncontradicted line of authority makes two propositions clear. The first is that the prosecution must prove that the child defendant ... when doing [the] act knew that it was a wrong act as distinct from an act of mere naughtiness or childish mischief ...

The second clearly established proposition is that the evidence to prove the defendant's guilty knowledge, as defined above, must not be the mere proof of the doing of the act charged, however horrifying or obviously wrong that act may be.

Extract from the Crime and Disorder Act 1998 (s34)

34. Abolition of rebuttable presumption that a child is *doli incapax*

The rebuttable presumption of criminal law that a child aged 10 or over is incapable of committing a crime is hereby abolished.

> **Read the three extracts above and answer the questions**
>
> **Questions:**
>
> 1. What does the first extract tell us about children who commit crimes?
> 2. What is the connection between the second extract and the third?

13.2 Insanity

Extract adapted from 'Mad or bad – the dilemma of insanity', Dr Gary Slapper, *The Times*, 8 December 1998

Care in the community has failed ...

Only last month the stabbing of a social worker at a South London hostel for psychiatric patients raised the issue of how the law should deal with people who commit crimes while suffering from clinical mental conditions.

Nowhere is the 'mad or bad' dichotomy reflected in a more confused way than in the criminal law's approach to insanity. For some people it is curious that the perpetrators of terrible crimes can be seen as anything other than psychotic and in need of treatment. In what circumstances can a deranged and savage person be judged as 'normal' then simply thrown in front of a judge and jury in an ordinary criminal trial, and convicted and punished?

Mental illness is a huge social problem. One in ten of us will at some time suffer a mental disorder. More than 50 people in Britain have been murdered by the mentally ill since 1993.

Kenneth McCaskill thought that he was the devil when he killed his father with a 12-inch kitchen knife, and then stabbed his mother. Yet in Edinburgh last month, McCaskill, whose condition was diagnosed as schizophrenia, was acquitted by a jury on the basis that he was 'not guilty by reason of insanity'. He will thus be sent to a secure mental institution.

By contrast, Michael Stone was last month jailed for life for the murders of Lin and Megan Russell. Stone had a history of mental illness, and before the killings had requested hospital treatment (which had been denied).

Criminal law on insanity is based on 19th century legal and medical assumptions. There have been calls for radical change of the rule but the law is still in a mould of outdated thinking. At the core of the problems are the different criteria of madness preferred in law and psychiatry.

Lord Lloyd recently highlighted the awkward relationship between the law and psychiatry. Sometimes, Parliament can legislate without envisaging that 'an existing psychiatric disorder might be regarded as treatable today and untreatable tomorrow owing to a change in psychiatric thinking'.

The basis of the law on insanity, which permits the insane to be found not guilty of any crime because of their condition, is that such people are not responsible for their actions. If a toddler pushes a brick out of a window and it kills someone, we do not presume to prosecute the child because it is not responsible for its actions or their consequences. The same reasoning applies to acquit the insane.

The guiding principles of insanity in law are found in the M'Naghten Rules, which arose from a case in 1843. M'Naghten had shot and killed a man whom he believed was Robert Peel, the Home Secretary. He had acted under a 'morbid delusion' that he was being persecuted by the police at the Government's behest.

There was political disquiet at his acquittal. The judges formulated a new set of rules starting with the proposition that every man is presumed to be sane and responsible for his crimes. The defence of insanity would only be open to someone who, at the time of a crime was 'labouring under such a defect of reason, from disease of the mind, as not to know the nature and quality of his act; or if he did know it, that he did not know that what he was doing was wrong'.

In cases of 1984 and 1989, the definition was held to cover epilepsy and a certain sort of diabetic problem.

It is remarkable that, at a time when so many patients are receiving 'care in the community', insanity (the only appropriate defence they can use if accused of a crime), is successfully used by defendants less than 20 times a year. A Royal Commission on capital punishment in 1953 deemed the M'Naghten Rules 'obsolete and misleading'. Unfortunately, nothing fundamental in the insanity laws has changed since.

Extract adapted from the judgment in *R v Quick; R v Paddison* [1973] QB 910, CA

Facts

Quick was a charge nurse in a mental hospital. He was convicted of giving a patient two black eyes, a fractured nose, a split lip requiring three stitches, and bruising to the arm and shoulders. Quick, a diabetic, admitted having eaten very little and also having drunk alcohol, and claimed to remember nothing of the assault. Quick pleaded guilty when the trial judge ruled that this evidence did not support Quick's defence of automatism and could only be used in a plea of insanity. His appeal was allowed on the error in this judgement.

Judgment

LAWTON LJ:

[In] hypoglycaemia, which is a condition brought about when there is more insulin in the bloodstream than the amount of sugar there can cope with ... [an] imbalance occurs [and] the higher functions of the mind are affected. In the later stages of mental impairment a sufferer may become aggressive and violent without being able to control himself or without knowing at the time what he was doing ... The question remains ... whether a mental condition arising from hypoglycaemia does amount to a disease of the mind ...

A malfunctioning of the mind of transitory [temporary] effect caused by the application to the body of some external factor such as violence, drugs, alcohol and hypnotic influences cannot fairly be said to be due to disease. Such malfunctioning, unlike that caused by a defect of reason from disease of the mind, will not always relieve ... criminal responsibility ... A self-induced incapacity will not excuse ...

Quick's alleged mental condition ... was not caused by his diabetes but by his use of the insulin ... [Any] malfunctioning of his mind ... was caused by an external factor and not by a bodily disorder in the nature of a disease which disturbed the working of his mind. ... Quick was entitled to have his defence of automatism left to the jury.

Read the two extracts above and answer the questions

Questions:

1. What is the effect of a successful plea of 'insanity'?
2. What does Dr Slapper say is the major problem in the law's treatment of insanity?
3. Why is an insane person who kills to be considered in the same way as a very young child who kills might be?
4. What sorts of defects can you identify in the basic M'Naghten Rules?
5. What possible alternatives could be used instead of the present test?
6. What is the difference between a hyperglycaemic state and a hypoglycaemic state, and what effect does the difference have on available defences?
7. Why was Quick's case not one of insanity?

13.3 Non-insane automatism

Extract adapted from the judgment in *Bratty v Attorney General for Northern Ireland* [1963] AC 386, HL

Facts

The appellant strangled a girl. He said in his statement to the police that when he was with her he had a 'terrible feeling' and 'a sort of blackness' came over him. At the trial there was evidence that he might have been suffering from psychomotor epilepsy. To a charge of murder he raised three defences: automatism, lack of intent, and insanity. The judge refused to leave the first two to the jury and they rejected the third. He was convicted and his eventual appeal in the House of Lords was dismissed.

Judgment

LORD DENNING:

No act is punishable if it is done involuntarily: and an involuntary act in this context – some people nowadays prefer to speak of it as 'automatism' – means an act ... done by the muscles without any control by the mind, such as a spasm, a reflex action or a convulsion; or an act done by a person who is not conscious of what he is doing, such as an act done whilst suffering from concussion or whilst sleepwalking ...

Extract adapted from the judgment in *R v Burgess* [1991] 2 QB 92, CA

The facts appear in the judgment

Judgment

LORD LANE CJ:

... the appellant was found not guilty by reason of insanity on a charge of wounding with intent [and] appeals against that verdict.

The appellant [hit the victim] on the head first with a bottle when she was asleep, then with a video recorder and finally grasping her round the throat.

His case was that he lacked the *mens rea* necessary to make him guilty of the offence because he was 'sleep-walking' ... he was suffering from non-insane automatism ...

Where the defence of automatism is raised by a defendant, two questions fall to be decided by the judge before the defence can be left to the jury. The first is whether a proper evidential foundation ... has been laid. The second is whether the evidence shows the case to be one of insane automatism, that is to say a case which falls within the M'Naghten rules, or one of non-insane automatism ...

The appellant plainly suffered from a defect of reason from some sort of failure of the mind causing him to act as he did without conscious motivation. His mind was to some extent controlling his actions which were purposive rather than the result of simple muscular spasm, but without his being consciously aware of what he was doing. Can it be said that that 'failure' was a *disease* of the mind rather than a defect or failure of the mind not due to disease? That is the distinction, by no means always easy to draw, upon which this case depends ...

[the] danger of recurrence ... may be an added reason for categorising the condition as a disease of the mind. On the other hand, the absence of the danger of recurrence is not a reason for saying that it cannot be a disease of the mind ... There have been several occasions when ... in the Court of Appeal and the House of Lords observations have been made, *obiter*, about the criminal responsibility of sleep-walkers, where sleep-walking has been used as a self-evident illustration of non-insane automatism. For example ... Lord Denning [said in *Bratty*]:

> 'The point was well put by Stephen J in 1899: "Can anyone doubt that a man who, though he might be perfectly sane, committed what would otherwise be a crime in a state of somnambulism, would be entitled to be acquitted?"'

[The doctor in the present case saw it as an] internal rather than ... external factor. He accepted that there is a liability to recurrence of sleep-walking. He could not go so far as to say that there is no liability of recurrence of serious violence ...

It seems to us on this evidence that the judge was right to conclude that this was an abnormality or disorder, albeit transitory, due to an internal factor, whether functional or organic, which had manifested itself in violence. It was a disorder or abnormality which might recur, though the possibility of it recurring in the form of serious violence was unlikely. Therefore, since this was a legal problem to be answered on legal principles the answer was as the judge found it to be. Appeal dismissed.

13.4 Intoxication

Extract adapted from the judgment in *DPP v Majewski* [1976] 2 WLR 623, HL

Facts

The defendant was convicted for assault, having attacked people in a public house and then the police officers who tried to arrest him. He had consumed large quantities of alcohol and drugs. His appeal on the ground that his intoxication prevented him from forming the necessary *mens rea* was also unsuccessful.

Judgment

LORD ELWYN-JONES LC:

Self-induced intoxication has been a factor in crimes of violence, like assault, throughout the history of crime in this country. But voluntary drug taking with the potential and actual dangers to others it may cause has added a new dimension to the old problem ... the crux of the case for the Crown was that, illogical as the outcome may be said to be, the judges have evolved for the purpose of protecting the community a substantive rule of law that, in crimes of basic intent as distinct from crimes of specific intent, self-induced intoxication provides no defence and is irrelevant to crimes of basic intent such, as assault.

The case for the appellant was that there was no such substantive rule of law and if there was, it did violence to logic and ethics and to fundamental principles of the criminal law which had been evolved to determine when and where criminal responsibility should arise.

If a man consciously and deliberately takes alcohol and drugs not on medical prescription, but in order to escape from reality, to go 'on a trip', to become hallucinated, whatever the description may be, and thereby disables himself from taking the care he might otherwise take and as a result by his subsequent actions causes injury to another – does our criminal law enable him to say that because he did not know what he was doing he lacked both intention and recklessness and accordingly is entitled to an acquittal?

Originally the common law would not and did not recognise voluntary intoxication as an excuse.

The authority which for the last half century has been relied on in this context has been the speech of Lord Birkenhead LC in *DPP v Beard*:

> 'Under the law of England as it prevailed until early in the nineteenth century voluntary drunkenness was never an excuse for criminal misconduct; and indeed the classic authorities broadly assert that voluntary drunkenness must be considered rather an aggravation than a defence.'

From this it seemed clear that it is only in the limited class of cases requiring proof of specific intent that drunkenness can exculpate. Otherwise in no case can it exempt completely from criminal liability.

I do not for my part regard that general principle as either unethical or contrary to the principles of natural justice. If a man of his own volition takes a substance which causes him to cast off the restraints of reason and conscience, no wrong is done to him by holding him answerable criminally for any injury he may do while in that condition. His course of conduct in reducing himself by drugs and drink to that condition in my view supplies the evidence of *mens rea*, of guilty mind certainly sufficient for crimes of basic intent. It is a reckless course of conduct and recklessness is enough to constitute the necessary *mens rea* in assault cases ...

Extract adapted from 'Involuntary intoxication', Nicholas Reville, *The Legal Executive Journal* (1995) January L. Ex

The recent unanimous House of Lords ruling, delivered by Lord Mustill, in *Kingston*, that the absence of moral fault on the part of the accused is not sufficient in itself to negative the necessary mental elements of a crime, has important practical implications for legal advisers.

In *Kingston* it was held that an intent to commit an indecent assault is a 'criminal' intent even though it is formed in circumstances of loss of self control induced by a third party surreptitiously [secretly] administering soporific [sleep causing] drugs.

Mr Kingston had paedophiliac homosexual tendencies. Another man, P, arranged to blackmail him by photographing and audio-taping him in a compromising situation with a boy. P lured a boy of 15 to his flat, where he gave him what seemed an innocuous drink and some cannabis. The boy fell asleep and remembered nothing until he woke the next morning.

While the boy was in this state, P invited Mr Kingston to abuse the boy sexually. He did so, and was photographed and taped doing it. Both Mr Kingston and P were charged with indecent assault on the boy.

Mr Kingston's defence was that P had laced his drink [and] had no recollection of events that night and had woken in his own home the next morning.

The House of Lords found that the induced mental condition on which Mr Kingston relied was disinhibition. His conviction implied that whatever drug he may have involuntarily taken had not such an effect on his mind that he did not intend to do what he did.

The taking of the drug lowered his ability to resist temptation, in that his desires overrode his ability to control them. The drug was not alleged to have created the desire but rather to have enabled it to be released.

The proposition that criminal liability should not be imposed on conduct which is the ultimate consequence of an event outside the defendant's volition is appealing. However, the harshness of the *Kingston* principle can be explained.

It would be difficult to reconcile a defence of irresistible impulse derived from a combination of innate drives and external disinhibition with the rule that irresistible impulse of a solely internal origin does not in itself excuse.

Equally, the state of mind which founds such a defence superficially resembles diminished responsibility. The effect in law is quite different.

There are also serious practical problems. Before a jury could form an opinion on whether the drug might have turned the scale, witnesses would have to give a picture of the defendant's personality.

More significant than this, the House of Lords felt in *Kingston*, would be the opportunities for a spurious defence.

The defendant would only have to assert, and support by the evidence of well wishers, that he was not the sort of person to have done this kind of thing.

In *Kingston*, the House of Lords felt that disinhibition should be a mitigating factor ... not a defence. This best recognised the interplay between the wrong done

Looking at Criminal Law

to the victim, the individual characteristics of the defendant and the pharmacological effects of whatever drug may be potentially involved.

Clearly a loss of self control through the acts of a third party do not now generally constitute a defence.

Consequently, provided the intoxication is not such as to cause automatism or temporary insanity, involuntary intoxication or disinhibition is not a defence to a criminal charge if it is proved that the defendant had the necessary intent when the necessary act was done by him. It is immaterial that the intent arose out of circumstances for which he was not to blame.

If, however, the defendant was so intoxicated that he could not form an intent, he has a defence.

Read the two extracts above and answer the questions

Questions:

1. In what way would we expect a defence of intoxication to work?
2. How does Elwyn-Jones LC in *Majewski* suggest that the defence of intoxication differs between crimes of specific intent and crimes of basic intent?
3. In what way does he also suggest that voluntary intoxication supplies sufficient *mens rea* for a crime?
4. What in the article on *Kingston* is said to have been the basis of *Kingston's* argument why he should not be convicted?
5. Why did this argument not succeed?
6. According to the article, when will a plea of involuntary intoxication be successful?

 Try this sample exam essay question:

Consider the extent to which, even though it has been reformed, the law on insanity is still in need of improvement.

Revision exercise:
WORDSEARCH: ON DEFENCES

Complete the Wordsearch below and you should find five words that are significant to defences and also five key cases.

They will be in a straight line but can be found running left to right or right to left, top to bottom or bottom to top, or diagonally up or down.

V	Y	R	A	T	N	U	L	O	V
A	B	B	A	R	I	N	G	T	O
N	A	I	T	I	S	T	N	L	L
D	S	A	R	M	S	R	I	U	U
D	I	S	I	N	O	U	T	B	N
N	C	S	O	A	M	E	R	I	T
I	I	O	N	G	N	A	R	I	J
M	N	M	O	H	T	W	E	T	I
E	T	N	O	T	S	G	N	I	K
H	E	A	Y	E	S	T	I	K	S
T	N	M	M	N	I	H	K	E	W
F	T	B	U	R	G	E	S	S	E
O	B	U	B	U	B	L	L	I	J
E	B	L	I	L	P	A	N	G	A
S	B	I	T	E	A	P	I	N	M
A	B	S	I	S	T	E	D	O	E
E	L	M	E	N	T	A	R	V	L
S	L	E	E	R	Y	P	I	N	C
I	N	I	F	F	D	D	D	V	V
D	R	I	V	E	L	L	I	L	I

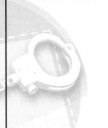

Besides defences that succeed because of the incapacity of the defendant, there are also general defences that succeed usually because they are seen as a valid excuse or justification for the crime. For instance, mistake, duress and necessity are all excuses made for a particular class of conduct, whereas in self-defence and, in rare circumstances necessity, the crime is seen as a justified response.

Duress

Extract adapted from the judgment in *R v Howe* [1987] 1 AC 417, HL

Facts

Howe and another man, Bannister, took part in the torturing and abusing of another man who was then strangled by a further man. Following the torture of another man on another occasion they this time strangled and killed the victim. They did so, they said, because they acted under threats of violence: duress. They were convicted for the second murder though the defence of duress was allowed in respect of the first murder where they were accessories. In their failed House of Lords appeal it was considered that duress should not be available to an accessory to murder either.

Judgment

LORD HAILSHAM LC:
A long line of cases establish duress as an available defence in a wide range of crimes.

I believe that some degree of proportionality between the threat and the offence must, at least to some extent, be a prerequisite of the defence under existing law. Few would resist threats to the life of a loved one if the alternative were driving across the red lights or in excess of 70 m.p.h. on the motorway. But it would take rather more than the threat of a slap on the wrist or even moderate pain or injury to discharge the evidential burden even in the case of a fairly serious assault. In such a case the 'concession to human frailty' is no more than to say that in such circumstances a reasonable man of average courage is entitled to embrace as a matter of choice the alternative which a reasonable man could regard as the lesser of two evils. Other considerations necessarily arise where the choice is between ... death or ... serious injury and deliberately taking an innocent life. In such a case a reasonable man might reflect that one innocent human life is at least as valuable as his own or that of his loved one. In such a case a man cannot claim that he is choosing the lesser of two evils. Instead he is embracing the cognate but morally disreputable principle that the end justifies the means.

LORD GRIFFITHS:
It is therefore neither rational nor fair to make the defence dependent upon whether the accused is the actual killer or took some other part in the murder.

As I can find no fair and certain basis on which to differentiate between participants to a murder and as I am firmly convinced that the law should not be extended to the killer, I would depart from the decision of this House in *DPP for Northern Ireland v Lynch* and declare the law to be that duress is not available as a defence to a charge of murder, or to attempted murder.

Extract adapted from the judgment in *R v Shepherd* (1988) 86 Cr App Rep 47, CA

Facts

The defendant joined a gang of shoplifters who stole while one member of the gang distracted the shopkeeper. The trial judge rejected his plea of duress, that he had wanted to give up after the first time but had been forced to continue by threats of violence. He succeeded on appeal.

Judgment

MUSTILL LJ:
(1) Although it is not easy to rationalise ... duress as a defence ... it must ... be founded on a concession to human frailty ... where the defendant has been faced with a choice between two evils.

(2) The exception which exists where the defendant has voluntarily allied himself with the person who exercises the duress must be founded on the assumption that, just as he cannot complain if he had the opportunity to escape the duress and failed to take

it, equally no concession to frailty is required if the risk of the duress is freely undertaken.

(3) Thus in some instances it will follow inevitably that the defendant has no excuse: for example, if he has joined a group of people dedicated to violence ... or overtly ready to use violence ...

(4) Other cases will be difficult ... there are certain kinds of criminal enterprises the joining of which, in the absence of any knowledge of propensity to violence ... would not lead another to suspect that a decision to think better of the whole affair might lead him into serious trouble ... if trouble did unexpectedly materialise, and if it put the defendant into a dilemma, in which a reasonable man might have chosen to act as he did, the concession to human frailty should not be denied to him.

Read the two extracts above and answer the questions

Questions:

1. In *Howe*, what do you think Lord Hailsham means by 'a concession to human frailty'?
2. What are the limitations to a successful plea of defence, according to Lord Hailsham in that case?
3. What important aspect of the defence is identified in Lord Griffiths' judgment?
4. How does Lord Mustill in *Shepherd* justify creating an exception to the availability of duress as a defence, and what exception does he apply to his own exception?

 14.2 Duress of circumstances

Extract adapted from the judgment in *Pommell* [1995] 2 Cr App R 607

Facts

The defendant was convicted of possessing a prohibited weapon. He was found in bed one morning with a loaded gun in his hand. He claimed that he had taken it from another man and had intended to hand it in to the police the next day. The court rejected his defence of duress of circumstances because of the delay, but the Court of Appeal allowed his appeal. The delay was not excessive and had been explained in this case.

Judgment

KENNEDY LJ:

The strength of the argument that a person ought to be permitted to breach the letter of the criminal law in order to prevent a greater evil [to] himself or others has long been recognised ... but has, in English law, not given rise to a general defence of necessity, and ... to ... murder, the defence has been specifically held not to exist (see *Dudley and Stephens*) ... Even in relation to other offences there are powerful arguments against recognising the general defence ...

However, that does not really deal with the situation where someone commendably infringes a regulation in order to prevent another person from committing what everyone would accept as being a greater evil with a gun. In that situation it cannot be satisfactory to leave it to the prosecuting authority not to prosecute ...

... in the present case the defence was open to the appellant ... [but] a person who has taken possession of a gun in circumstances where he has the defence of duress of circumstances must 'desist from committing the crime as soon as he reasonably can' ...

Extract adapted from the judgment in *R v Martin* [1989] 88 Cr App R 343, CA

Facts

Martin was convicted of driving while disqualified. He claimed that his wife had suicidal tendencies and that, on the occasion in question, she had threatened to commit suicide unless he drove his stepson to work. The boy had overslept and would be late for work otherwise. There was evidence of his wife's previous attempts at suicide, and a doctor considered that on the day in question, in view of her general state, it was likely that she may have attempted suicide again. On appeal, Martin succeeded in demonstrating this claim and his appeal was allowed and the conviction quashed.

Judgment

SIMON BROWN J:

The appellant's case on the facts was that he genuinely, and he would suggest reasonably, believed that his wife would carry out the threat unless he did as she demanded. Despite his disqualification he therefore drove the boy.

Sceptically though one may regard that defence on the facts the sole question before this court is whether those facts, had the jury accepted they were or might be true, amounted in law to a defence. As it was, such a defence was pre-empted by the ruling. Should it have been?

In our judgment the answer is plainly not. The authorities are now clear.

The principles may be summarised thus. ... English law does, in extreme circumstances, recognise a defence of necessity. Most commonly this defence arises as duress. Equally, however, it can arise from other objective dangers threatening the accused or others. Arising thus it is conveniently called 'duress of circumstances'.

Secondly, the defence is available only if, from an objective standpoint, the accused can be said to be acting reasonably and proportionately in order to avoid a threat of death or serious injury.

Thirdly, the issue should be left to the jury, who should be directed to determine these two questions: first was the accused, or may he have been, impelled to act as he did because as a result of what he reasonably believed to be the situation he had good cause to fear that otherwise death or serious physical injury would result? Second, if so, would a sober person of reasonable firmness, sharing the characteristics of the accused, have responded to that situation by acting as the accused acted? If the answer to both those questions was Yes, then the jury would acquit; the defence of necessity would have been established.

14.3 Necessity

Extract adapted from the judgment in *Re A (Conjoined Twins)* [2000] *NLJ* Law Reports, 6 October 2000, pp 1453–1454

Facts

J and M were conjoined twins ... J was capable of independent existence, but an operation to separate the twins would inevitably have resulted in the death of M who was alive only because a common artery enabled her sister to circulate oxygenated blood for both of them. If there was no such operation they would both die ... The parents would not consent ..., but the doctors were convinced that they could carry out the operation so as to give J a life that would be worthwhile. The Trust therefore sought a declaration confirming the lawfulness of the proposed operation.

Judgment

WARD LJ:
The judge was plainly right to conclude that the operation would be in J's best interest. The question was whether it would be in M's best interest. It could not be. It would bring her life to an end before its natural span. It denied her inherent right to life.

A balance had to be struck ... The best interests of the twins was to give the chance of life to the twin whose actual bodily condition was capable of accepting the chance to her advantage even if that had to be at the cost of the sacrifice of the life which was so unnaturally supported. This was, however, subject to whether what was proposed to be done could be lawfully done.

The crucial question was whether the law should confer in any circumstances, however extreme, the right to choose that one innocent person should be killed rather than another.

... the doctors could not be denied a right of choice if they were under a duty to choose. They were under a duty to M not to operate because it would kill M, but they were under a duty to J to operate because not to do so would kill her. It was important to stress that it made no difference whether the killing was by act or omission.

In those circumstances the law had to allow an escape through choosing the lesser of the two evils. Faced as they were with an apparently irreconcilable conflict the doctors should be in no different position from that in which the court itself was placed ... giving the sanctity of life principle its place in the balancing exercise that had to be undertaken. For the same reasons that led to the conclusion that consent should be given to operate, the conclusion had to be that the carrying out of the operation would be justified as the lesser evil and no unlawful act would be committed.

Extract adapted from 'The Manchester Conjoined Twins Case', Christopher F. Sharp QC, *New Law Journal*, 6 October 2000, pp 1460–1462

The issue for the court was whether an act by the doctors which, while saving Jodie's life, and although not primarily intended to kill Mary, would have that inevitable effect, would be unlawful or could be justified ... This led finally to a detailed consideration of the doctrine of necessity.

The Court's approach was to accept that the doctrine of necessity, which in its related form of duress has been rejected by the House of Lords in *Howe* ... as a defence to murder, ... could nevertheless in the unique circumstances of this case be extended to cover the doctors' intended action ... Robert Walker LJ concluded that in the absence of Parliamentary intervention the law as to the defence is going to have to develop on a case by case basis ... and this was an appropriate case to extend it, if necessary.

Ward LJ having identified the rationale of the rejection of the defence of necessity as one based on the sanctity of life, and having identified as the crucial question in this case the question posed by Lord Mackay in *Howe* whether the circumstances could ever be extreme enough for the law to confer a right to choose that one innocent person should be killed rather than another, held that ... the law should allow an escape by permitting the doctors to choose the lesser of two evils.

Brooke LJ carried out an exhaustive review of the jurisprudence ... From ... Stephen, he derived three necessary requirements for the application of the doctrine:

   (i) the act is needed to avoid inevitable and irreparable evil;

   (ii) no more should be done than is reasonably necessary for the purpose to be achieved;

   (iii) the evil inflicted must not be disproportionate to the evil avoided.

Given that the ... law pointed irresistibly to the conclusion that the interests of Jodie must be preferred to the conflicting interests of Mary, he considered that all three of these requirements were satisfied in this case.

Read the four extracts in the two sections above and answer the questions below

Questions:

1. Looking at *Martin*, what connections can be seen with the defence of duress?
2. When will a defence of 'duress of circumstances' be successful?
3. In *Pommell*, what are Lord Justice Kennedy's justifications for allowing the defence of duress of circumstances?
4. In *Re A* what does Lord Justice Ward recognise as the dilemma facing the doctors because of their duty as doctors?
5. In Sharp's article, what does Lord Justice Brooke recognise as the requirements necessary for a defence of necessity to be lawfully applied?

14.4 Mistake

Extract adapted from 'Mistake, strict liability and the criminal law – Part 2', John Beaumont, *New Law Journal*, 24 March 2000

[Facts repeated from the first article which can be found in Chapter 2, Section 2.4. – Strict liability offences]:

I[n] *B V DPP*...The defendant was charged with inciting a girl aged under fourteen to commit an act of gross indecency with him contrary to s1(1) of the Indecency with Children Act 1960.

A girl aged 13 was a passenger on a bus The defendant, who was 15, sat next to her. He asked her to perform oral sex with him. She refused. He repeated his request several times and she repeatedly refused. It was accepted that the defendant honestly believed that the girl was over 14.]

... on the second question ... mistake ... Lord Nicholls started by drawing attention to the traditional approach to this question, whereby in the case of a defendant who had acted under a mistaken view of the facts, such an honest mistake did not avail him, unless it had been made on reasonable grounds. Another case ... *Tolson* where on a charge of bigamy the defendant mistakenly believed that her husband was dead at the time of the second ceremony, is ... one authority ... for this ... approach. However, in the last 25 years the implications of the subjective nature of ... mens rea have come to be recognised [notably] in *Morgan*, [where] it was held that in a case of rape an honest belief in consent, even if not based on reasonable grounds, is a defence. The question as to whether the 'honest belief' approach ... in *Morgan* applied generally in the criminal law, or ... had only limited application was at first unclear [with] at least two important issues in a state of uncertainty. The first was whether the honest belief approach applied to cases where the statute in question did not use words expressing a criminal element [as] in *Tolson*.

The second was whether the honest belief approach applied to mistakes as to a matter of defence. *Morgan* concerned ... mistake as to something that was expressly part of the definition of the crime itself, rather than a mistake as to a defence ...

The status of cases [such as] *Tolson* were in doubt after *Morgan*. That they are unsound would seem inevitably to follow from ... *B v DPP*. This is because Lord Nicholls' summary of the application of mistake ... is put in general terms and not specified as subject to any specific exceptions.

'... the honest belief approach must be preferable. By definition, the mental element in a crime is concerned with a subjective state of mind, such as intent or belief ... The traditional formulation of the common law presumption, in so far as it envisaged that a mistaken belief had to be based on reasonable grounds, was out of step with recent authority.'

... the person who deliberately kills another person mistaking the profession of the victim is making a mistake that is irrelevant to the question of his liability. ... In the hunting case [mistaking the victim for an animal] the defendant's defence would operate in the normal way to give him a defence to murder, since he does not intend to kill or do grievous bodily harm to a human being.

When it comes to the case of mistaken self-defence, again the basic principles apply and if the defendant's mistake is an honest one, ... defence is available, even if his defence is not ... on reasonable grounds.

As far as mistake as to the criminal law ... this is generally no defence, since usually knowledge that the act is forbidden ... is no part of the *mens rea* and ... the defendant cannot be said to lack *mens rea* ...

B v DPP is ... a landmark in the criminal law. Their Lordships grasped the ... principle with both hands and sidelined two cases that have long exerted considerable authority ... *Prince* and *Tolson*. [so] the court has been able to go on and endorse an almost fully subjectivist approach to ... *mens rea*.

Read the extract above and answer the questions below

Questions:

1. A mistake as to what will be accepted as a defence in the criminal law?
2. And a mistake as to what will not be accepted as a defence?
3. What word characterises a mistake amounting to a defence?
4. Why is *B v DPP* an important case?

14.5 Self-defence

Extract adapted from 'Self-defence or assault?', Penny Lewis, *The Times*, Tuesday, 9 May 2000

Two weeks after Tony Martin's conviction for shooting dead a burglar at his Norfolk home the case is becoming a cause célèbre. While the outcome of his appeal [has] implications for Martin, people want to know what to do if they come face to face with an intruder.

According to the law, a person who acts in reasonable self-defence commits no unlawful act. The right to protect oneself and others is set out in section 3 of the Criminal Law Act 1967, which mirrors the previous common law position. This says that 'a person may use

such force as is reasonable in all the circumstances in the prevention of crime or in effecting or assisting in the lawful arrest of offenders or of persons unlawfully at large.' But what is reasonable force?

Some believe that a homeowner has carte blanche to act as he pleases to defend the property. This is incorrect. In practice it is likely that the tables will only be turned on the 'victim' who tackles an assailant if serious injury or death results. Common sense dictates that this is more likely with the use of offensive weapons.

The leading authority on self-defence is ... *Palmer v R (1971)*. Lord Morris said that the test for the jury was whether the defendant's response was proportionate to the danger. This simple formula reflects the need for the accused to have acted reasonably, making all due allowances for panic, the element of surprise and the need to act on the spur of the moment.

Importantly, the judge refrained from providing an exhaustive list of acceptable responses, acknowledging that each case turns upon its own facts. Accordingly the outcome is dependent upon the standards of the community and whether the jury shares the prevailing public opinions. The judge acknowledged that 'it is both good law and common sense that a man who is attacked may defend himself ... but may only do what is reasonably necessary'.

The controversy surrounding the Martin case is largely because the concept of self-defence applies only where someone is either attacked or in danger. However upsetting it may be to know that robbers are ransacking your home, you are not allowed to initiate violence unless you genuinely fear that if you do not get in first you will come to harm. If you choose to attack in anger ... you will expose yourself to prosecution.

Questions:

1. What things may be protected under the defence of self-defence or prevention of crime?
2. What defeated Martin's chance to use the defence?

 Try this sample A Level exam essay:

Discuss the extent to which it is appropriate that the courts have limited the availability of the defence of duress.

Revision exercise:
MULTIPLE CHOICE CASE QUIZ

In each of the following lists of cases 1–10 one or more cases are fictitious. Identify which cases are real by placing a tick in the middle box. Then identify in the right-hand box from which general defence the case comes. You should also use the activity to try to remember the significance of the case.

1	D v PBB P v BDD B v DPP		
2	R v How R v Howe R v Why		
3	R v Swineherd R v Goatherd R v Shepherd		
4	Moron v DPP Moran v DPP Morgan v DPP		
5	R v Sweet R v Sharp R v Sour		
6	Nasser Hussain Abdul Hussain Abdul Rama		
7	Graham & Taylor Hudson & Hawk Hudson & Taylor		
8	R v Pummel R v Pumice R v Pommell		
9	R v Kitchen R v Kitson R v Kitsoff		
10	Beckham Beckford Beckwith		

CHAPTER 15

PARTICIPATION

'Principals' generally carry out crimes but there can also be secondary parties who support or assist. The question is what degree of involvement leads to participation and possible conviction as an accomplice. A further problem concerns joint enterprise. What happens if two people set out to carry out one crime but another, possibly more serious, is committed by one party and the other knew this was a possible outcome?

Secondary participation

Extract from the Accessories and Abettors Act 1861 (s8)

8. Abettors in misdemeanours

Whosoever shall aid, abet, counsel or procure the commission of [any indictable offence], whether the same be at common law or by virtue of any Act passed or to be passed, shall be liable to be tried, indicted, and punished as a principal offender.

Extract adapted from the judgment in *Attorney-General's Reference (No 1 of 1975)* [1975] 2 All ER 684, CA

Facts
The accused laced his friend's drink with spirits, knowing the friend had to drive home. The friend did drive and was convicted for drink driving. The reference concerned whether an accused could claim no case to answer, with no positive encouragement by the accused to the driver to drive with excess alcohol in his blood.

Judgment

LORD WIDGERY CJ:
The language in the section which determines whether a 'secondary party' ... is guilty of a criminal offence committed by another embraces the four words 'aid, abet, counsel or procure'.

... in the great majority of instances where a secondary party is sought to be convicted of an offence there has been a contact between the principal offender and the secondary party. Aiding and abetting almost inevitably involves a situation in which the secondary party and the main offender are together at some stage discussing the plans which they may be making in respect of the alleged offence, and are in contact so that each knows what is in the mind of the other.

In the same way ... a person who counsels the commission of a crime of another, almost inevitably comes to a moment when he is in contact with that other, when he is discussing the offence with that other and when, to use the words of the statute, he counsels the other to commit the offence.

The fact that so often the relationship between the secondary party and the principal will be such that there is a meeting of minds between them caused the trial judge in the case to think that this was really an essential feature of proving or establishing the guilt of the secondary party and, he took the view that in the absence of some sort of meeting of minds, there could be no aiding, abetting or counselling of the offence within the meaning of the section.

So far as aiding, abetting and counselling is concerned we would go a long way with that conclusion. But we do not see why a similar principle should apply to procuring. ... if four words are employed ... the probability is that there is a difference between each ... because, if there were no ... difference, ... Parliament would [not] waste time ... using four words where two or three would do.

To procure means to produce by endeavour. [i.e.] to see that it happens and taking the appropriate steps to produce this happening. ... there are plenty of instances in which a person may be said to procure the commission of a crime by another even though there is no ... conspiracy ..., even though there is no attempt at agreement or [as to] the form which the offence should take. ... [as here].

[Here] the accused surreptitiously laced his friend's drink. This is an important element ... the conception of another procuring the commission of the offence by the driver is very much stronger where the driver is innocent of all knowledge of what is happening, as in the present case where the lacing of the drink was surreptitious.

The second thing which is important ... is that following and in consequence of the introduction of the extra alcohol, the friend drove with an excess quantity of alcohol in his blood. Causation here is important. You cannot procure an offence unless there is a causal link between what you do and the commission of the offence, and here we are told that in consequence of the addition of this alcohol the driver ... drove with an excess quantity of alcohol in his body.

... the offence has been procured ...

Extract adapted from the judgment in *R v Coney* [1882] 8 QBD 534

Facts
Convictions of spectators at an illegal prize-fight for aiding and abetting were quashed by the Court for Crown Cases Reserved since there was no evidence that they encouraged the fighters. Mere presence was insufficient.

Judgment

HAWKINS J:
... to constitute an aider and abettor some active steps must be taken by word or action, with the intent to instigate the principal[s]. Encouragement does not ... amount to aiding and abetting, it may be intentional or unintentional, a man may unwittingly encourage another in fact by his presence, by misinterpreted words, or gestures, or by his silence or non-interference, or ... encourage intentionally by expressions, gestures, or actions intended to signify approval. In the latter case he aids and abets, in the former he does not. It is no criminal offence to stand by, a mere passive spectator of a crime, even of murder.

Non-interference to prevent a crime is not in itself a crime. [it] might [sometimes] afford genuine evidence upon which a jury would be justified in finding that he wilfully encouraged and so aided and abetted.

Read the three extracts above and answer the questions

Questions:

1. What are the different ways of acting as an accomplice?
2. According to Lord Widgery in the *Attorney-General's Reference*, in what way do they differ from one another?
3. What feature is usually common to both aiding and abetting?
4. Why is it not necessary for a procurer to communicate directly with the principal?
5. What feature does Lord Widgery suggest is the most vital element of procuring?

 15.2

Joint venture

Extract adapted from the judgment in *R v Powell and Another; R v English [1997]* 4 All ER 545, HL

Facts
The case involved joint appeals on joint enterprise.

Powell and Daniels and another went to purchase drugs from a dealer, [the] joint enterprise. The dealer was shot dead and the Crown could not prove which man fired the shot. The Crown's case was that the other two were guilty of murder in any case as they knew that the third man was armed and realised that he might use the gun and kill or seriously injure the drug dealer. They were convicted and [failed in] their appeal.

The joint enterprise between English and Weddle was to attack a police officer with wooden posts. During the attack Weddle killed the policeman with a knife. English possibly had no knowledge of the knife but the trial judge directed that he could be convicted of murder if he knew that there was a substantial risk that death or serious injury might be caused with the wooden post. English was convicted and his appeal rejected by the Court of Appeal.

Powell and Daniels' appeals were rejected [since] they knew that the primary party might kill or cause serious injury ... English's appeal was granted on the basis that the lethal act by Weddle was fundamentally different from the act that he foresaw.

Judgment

LORD HUTTON:
The first issue is whether there is a principle established in the authorities that where there is a joint enterprise to commit a crime, foresight or contemplation that by one party to the enterprise that another party to the enterprise may in the course of it commit another crime, is sufficient to impose criminal liability for that crime if committed by the other party even if the first party did not intend that criminal act to be carried out.

… there is a strong line of authority that where two parties embark on a joint enterprise … and one party foresees that in the course of the enterprise the other party may carry out, with the requisite *mens rea*, an act constituting another crime, the former is liable for that crime if committed by the latter in the course of the enterprise.

… in *R v Smith* the Court of Appeal recognised that the secondary party will be guilty of unlawful killing committed by the primary party … if he contemplates … the primary party may use such a weapon.

As a matter of strict analysis there is, as Professor Smith pointed out, a distinction between a party to a common enterprise contemplating that in the course of the enterprise another party may use a gun or a knife and a party tacitly agreeing that in the course of the enterprise another party may use such a weapon. However, it is clear from a number of decisions that … when two parties embark on a joint criminal enterprise one party will be liable for an act which he contemplates may be carried out by the other party in the course of the enterprise even if he has not tacitly agreed to the act.

The second issue which arises on these appeals is whether the line of authority exemplified by *R v Smith* is good law in the light of the decisions of this House in *R v Moloney* and *R v Hancock*. In reliance upon [those cases] the appellants submitted that as a matter of principle there is an anomaly in requiring proof against a secondary party of a lesser *mens rea* than needs to be proved against the principal who commits the *actus reus* of murder. If foreseeability of risk is insufficient to found the *mens rea* of murder for a principal then the same test of liability should apply in the case of a secondary party to the joint enterprise.

I recognise that as a matter of logic there is force in the argument … and that on one view it is anomalous that if foreseeability of death or really serious harm is not sufficient to constitute *mens rea* for murder in the party who actually carries out the killing, it is sufficient to constitute *mens rea* in a secondary party. But the rules of the common law are not based solely on logic but relate to practical concerns …

There is, in my opinion, an argument of considerable force that the secondary party who takes part in a criminal enterprise with foresight that a deadly weapon may be used, should not escape liability for murder because he, unlike the principal party, is not suddenly confronted by the security officer so that he has to decide whether to use the gun or knife …

Therefore for the reasons which I have given … it is sufficient to found a conviction for murder for a secondary party to have realised that in the course of the joint enterprise the primary party might kill with intent to do so or with intent to cause grievous bodily harm. Accordingly I would dismiss the appeals.

The second certified question in the appeal of English arises because of the trial judge's summing up.

The appellant advanced the submission that in a case such as the present one where the primary party kills with a deadly weapon which the secondary party did not know that he had and therefore did not foresee his use of it, the secondary party should not be guilty of murder.

I consider that this submission is correct.

Accordingly, in the appeal of English, I consider that the direction of the learned trial judge was defective because he did not qualify his direction on foresight of really serious injury by stating that if the jury considered that the use of the knife by Weddle was the use of a weapon and an action which English did not foresee as a possibility then English should not be convicted of murder.

On the evidence the jury could have found … English did not know … Weddle had a knife. [so] the judge's direction made the conviction unsafe and the appeal should be allowed.

Extract adapted from 'Manslaughter and accomplices', Laurence Toczek, *New Law Journal*, 22 September 2000

[If convicted] London nail bomber, David Copeland … had received assistance from another [and] that other realised that Copeland might plant bombs with the intention of killing or causing serious injury, he would have been guilty of murder. In *R v Powell* … the House of Lords dismissed [the] appeals, holding that an accomplice is guilty of murder where he realises that the principal might kill with intent to do so or with intent to cause grievous bodily harm.

… if the accomplice thought that Copeland's intention was only to cause fear … not to kill or seriously injure

... following *Powell*, the assistant would not have been guilty of murder [whether he would] have been guilty of involuntary manslaughter ... is not quite so clear [with] conflicting ... authority ...

In *R v Anderson and Morris* ... Anderson stabbed ... and killed [a man]. Morris said that he had not known that Anderson was going to use the knife. In quashing Morris's [manslaughter] conviction, the Court of Appeal [held] 'if one [party] goes beyond what has been ... agreed as part of the common enterprise, his co-adventurer is not liable for the ... unauthorised act.'

However, in *R v Stewart and Schofield* the defendants and a third man ... armed with a scaffolding pole agreed to rob a shop keeper. [They] realised that the third man might use the ... pole to frighten ... [In] the robbery ... the third man killed the shopkeeper with the scaffolding pole. The jury acquitted the two of murder but convicted them of manslaughter. They appealed on the basis that the killing was outside the scope of the joint enterprise. The Court of Appeal rejected this argument ...

In *Gilmour* the defendant drove three ... Protestant ... terrorists ... to a Catholic estate [where] two threw a petrol bomb [into] a house ... Three children died ...The defendant was convicted of murder. The Court of Appeal of Northern Ireland ... decided ... that, although the defendant knew a petrol bombing was planned, he did not realise that the principals would act with intention to inflict grievous bodily harm. The court held that where the principal carries out the very act contemplated by the accomplice, but with a different intention, the accomplice is guilty of the degree of offence appropriate to the intention with which he acted ... quashed the murder conviction and substituted one for manslaughter.

[In trying] to reconcile ... apparently conflicting ... cases. They said that ... *Anderson and Morris* dealt with the situation where the principal departed from the contemplated joint enterprise and perpetrated a more serious act of a different kind unforeseen by the accomplice. [But] in *Stewart and Schofield* and [*Gilmour*] the principal carried out the very act contemplated by the accomplice, although the latter did not realise that the principal intended a more serious consequence.

In *English* the defendant and another man attacked a police officer with wooden posts. The other man then ... stabbed the officer to death. The House of Lords quashed [English's] conviction [for murder] on the ground that even if he foresaw that the other man might act with intent to cause grievous bodily harm ... the use of a knife was a fundamentally different act.

Gilmour did not foresee grievous bodily harm, but he is liable ... English did foresee grievous bodily harm, but he is not liable ... this is an anomaly and an important one.

Read the two extracts above and answer the questions

Questions:

1. What were the joint enterprises in *Powell and Daniels* and in *English*?
2. Why were none of these parties principal offenders in the killings?
3. What does Lord Hutton say is 'sufficient to found a conviction for murder' in the case of a secondary participant?
4. Why were the appeals of Powell and Daniels decided differently to that of English?

 ### Try this sample A Level exam essay:

Critically consider the ways in which the courts have interpreted the words 'aiding', 'abetting', 'counselling' and 'procuring'.

Revision exercise:
PARTICIPATION CROSSWORD

Answer the clues 1–9 in the spaces in the crossword below to discover another way of describing this type of liability in the shaded line reading across

CLUES
1. Would someone in the Town Hall advise you on this?
2. Definitely not English, this appellant
3. By taking part, are you in favour of the medicine?
4. A little fashion extra or another person taking part!
5. Do we eat it together on Sundays?
6. Sounds like I'm being very helpful here!
7. Would I be an accomplice if I put it on a horse or a dog?
8. If we put in an ad ahead of it, it could be quite exciting
9. Producer of an important judgment on participation

These are incomplete crimes. There are three: attempt, conspiracy and incitement. Problems in attempt concern what amounts to something 'more than merely preparatory' and what happens when the defendant attempts the impossible. Conspiracy is now a statutory offence but there are still strange categories of conspiracy specifically retained as common-law offences by Parliament. Incitement is some form of encouragement to another to commit a crime which is then not actually carried out.

16.1 Attempt

Extract from the Criminal Attempts Act 1981 (s1)

1. Attempting to commit an offence

(1) If, with intent to commit an offence to which this section applies, a person does an act which is more than merely preparatory to the commission of the offence, he is guilty of attempting to commit the offence.

(2) A person may be guilty of attempting to commit an offence to which this section applies even though the facts are such that the commission of the offence is impossible.

(3) In any case where–
   (a) apart from this subsection a person's intention would not be regarded as having amounted to an intent to commit an offence; but
   (b) if the facts of the case had been as he believed them to be,
his intention would be so regarded.

Extract adapted from the judgment in *R v Campbell* [1991] 93 Cr App R 350, CA

Facts

Police, who had been tipped off that he was going to rob it, arrested Campbell outside a post office. Campbell had in his possession an imitation gun and a threatening note which he had planned to pass to the assistant. He was convicted of attempted robbery but appealed successfully because he had not done sufficient to amount to an attempt.

Judgment

WATKINS LJ:
Looking at the circumstances here it was beyond dispute that the appellant, at the material time, was carrying an imitation firearm which he made no attempt to remove from his clothing.

In order to effect the robbery it is equally beyond dispute it would have been quite impossible unless obviously he had entered the post office, gone to the counter and made some kind of hostile act – directed, of course, at whoever was behind the counter and in a position to hand him some money. A number of acts remained undone and the series of acts which he had already performed – were clearly acts which were, in the judgment of this court, indicative of mere preparation.

If a person, in circumstances such as this, has not even gained the place where he could be in a position to carry out the offence, it is extremely unlikely that it could ever be said that he had performed an act which could properly be said to be an attempt.

Extract adapted from the judgment in *R v Shivpuri* [1987] AC 1, HL

Facts

When arrested, Shivpuri believed that he was actually carrying large quantities of prohibited drugs. In fact, the substance that he was carrying was described later as 'harmless vegetable matter' and not drugs at all. He was convicted of attempting to be knowingly concerned in dealing with and harbouring Class A and Class B drugs. He appealed on the basis of the earlier decisions in *Haughton v Smith* and *Anderton v Ryan* that he could not be convicted of attempting a crime that was factually impossible for him to commit. His appeal in the House of Lords failed.

Judgment

LORD BRIDGE:

The first question to be asked is whether the appellant intended to commit the offences … did the appellant intend to receive and store (harbour) and in due course pass on to third parties (deal with) packages of heroin or cannabis which he knew had been smuggled into England from India? The answer is plainly yes, he did. Next, did he in relation to each offence, do an act which was more than merely preparatory to the commission of the offence? The act relied on in relation to harbouring was the receipt and retention of the packages found in the lining of the suitcase. The act relied on in relation to dealing was the meeting at Southall station with the intended recipient of one of the packages. In each case the act was clearly more than merely preparatory to the commission of the *intended* offence; it was not and could not be more than merely preparatory to the commission of the *actual* offence, because the facts were such that the commission of the actual offence was impossible. Here then is the nub of the matter. Does the 'act which is more than merely preparatory to the commission of the offence' in section 1(1) of the Act of 1981 (the *actus reus* of the statutory offence of attempt) require any more than an act which is more than merely preparatory to the commission of the offence which the defendant intended to commit? Section 1(2) must surely indicate a negative answer; if it were otherwise, whenever the facts were such that the commission of the actual offence was impossible, it would be impossible to prove an act more than merely preparatory to the commission of that offence and subsections (1) and (2) would contradict each other.

Read the three extracts above and answer the questions

Questions:

1. According to s 1(1) of the Act and the case of *Campbell*, how far towards the actual commission of the offence does an accused have to go in order to be guilty of attempting to commit the full offence?
2. Why precisely was *Campbell* not guilty of attempt?
3. What particular act on the part of the police might have made a difference?
4. What, according to the sources, is the necessary *mens rea* for the offence of attempt?
5. What does s1(3) tell us about attempt?
6. Why could *Shivpuri* not be guilty of dealing in or harbouring the prohibited drugs?
7. Why does Lord Bridge suggest that he can still be guilty of attempt?

Revision Exercise:
QUICK QUIZ: ATTEMPT PROBLEM

Consider whether I could be guilty of attempted burglary in the following example:

An accomplice has given me a set of keys to an off-licence in High Street, Low Town. Intending to steal large quantities of alcohol, I set off and arrive by mistake at the off-licence in Low Street, High Town. Police arrest me as I am puzzling over why the keys look far too big for the lock.

16.2 Conspiracy

Extract from the Criminal Law Act 1977 (s1(1), s2(1) and s2(2)) (as amended by the Criminal Attempts Act 1981)

1. The offence of conspiracy

(1) Subject to the following provisions of this part of this Act, if a person agrees with any other person or persons that a course of conduct shall be pursued which, if the agreement is carried out in accordance with their intentions, either–
   (a) will necessarily amount to or involve the commission of any offence or offences by one or more of the parties to the agreement;
   (b) would do so but for the existence of facts which render the commission of the offence or any of the offences impossible,
he is guilty of conspiracy to commit the offence or offences in question.

2. Exemptions from liability for conspiracy

(1) A person shall not by virtue of section 1 above be guilty of conspiracy to commit any offence if he is an intended victim of that offence.

(2) A person shall not by virtue of section 1 above be guilty of conspiracy to commit any offence or offences if the only other person or persons with whom he agrees are (both initially and at all times during the currency of the agreement) persons of any one or more of the following descriptions, that is to say–
   (a) his spouse;
   (b) a person under the age of criminal responsibility; and
   (c) an intended victim of that offence or of each of the offences.

Extract adapted from the judgment in *R v Anderson* [1986] AC 27, HL

Facts

The appellant agreed to supply diamond wire to a prisoner's brother to be used to cut through cell bars to escape. He claimed that he believed the plan had no chance of success and so lacked *mens rea* as to assisting in the escape. His appeal failed.

Judgment

LORD BRIDGE OF HARWICH:

... the elements of the new statutory offence of conspiracy must be ascertained purely by interpretation of the language of section 1(1) of the Act of 1977.

Clause (1) presents ... no difficulty. To be convicted the party charged must have agreed with one or more others that 'a course of conduct shall be pursued'.

Again Clause (2) could hardly use simpler language ... it is not necessary that more than one of the participants ... shall commit a substantive offence.

... only Clause (3) presents ... possible ambiguity ... the party charged should not only have agreed that a course of conduct be pursued [which] involves ... an offence ... but must also ... have intended that the offence should be committed.

... beyond the mere fact of agreement, the necessary *mens rea* of the crime is established only if it is shown that the accused, when he entered into the agreement, intended to play some part in the agreed course of conduct ...

Applying this test ... the appellant ... clearly intended, by providing diamond wire to be smuggled into the prison, to play a part in the agreed course of conduct ... Neither the fact that he intended to play no further part in attempting to effect the escape, nor that he believed the escape to be impossible, would ... have afforded him any defence.

Extract adapted from the judgment in *Knuller v DPP* [1973] AC 435, HL

Facts

The appellants published a magazine including a column headed 'Males' which was in fact a series of advertisements for contacting practising homosexuals. Their eventual appeal to the House of Lords, against conviction for conspiracy to corrupt public morals and for conspiracy to outrage public decency, was unsuccessful.

Judgment

LORD SIMON OF GLAISDALE:

... counsel for the appellants was right to concede that there is a common law offence of conspiring to outrage public decency.

... the substantive offence (and therefore the conduct the subject of the conspiracy) must be committed in public, in the sense that the circumstances must be such that the alleged outrageously indecent matter could have been seen by more than one person, even though in fact no more than one did see it.

... it would [not] necessarily negative the offence that the act or exhibit is superficially hid from view, if the public is expressly or impliedly invited to penetrate the cover.

Read the three extracts above and answer the questions

Questions:

1. Using the first two sources, what are the essential elements of a conspiracy?
2. With whom could I not conspire?
3. Why did Anderson's appeal fail?
4. What is the essential element of the conspiracy in *Knuller*? Why do you think Parliament preserved it as a common-law offence?

16.3 Incitement

Extract adapted from the judgment in *R v Fitzmaurice* [1983] QB 1083, CA

Facts

The appellant was asked by his father to find someone to rob a woman on her way to the bank. The appellant, believing an actual robbery was to take place, approached an unemployed man in need of money to take part in the robbery. In fact, the robbery was an invention of the father who intended to claim reward money for providing information. The appellant was convicted of incitement and appealed unsuccessfully on the ground that at common law incitement could not occur where it was impossible to commit the offence incited.

Judgment

NEILL J:

... the right approach in ... incitement is the same as

that ... underlined by Lord Scarman in *DPP v Nock* when he considered the offence of conspiracy. In every case it is necessary to analyse the evidence with care to decide the precise offence which the defendant is alleged to have incited ...

... where the committal of the specific offence is shown to be impossible it may be quite logical for the inciter to be convicted even though the alleged conspirators ... may be acquitted. On the other hand, if B and C agree to kill D, and A standing beside B and C, though not intending to take any active part whatever in their crime, encourages them [there is] no ... reason, if it turns out later that D was already dead, why A should be convicted of incitement ... whereas B and C ... would be entitled to an acquittal on a charge of conspiracy. The crucial question is to establish on the evidence the course of conduct which the alleged inciter was encouraging.

[In] the instant case ... the case against the appellant was based upon the steps he took to recruit Bonham. At that stage the appellant believed that there was to be a wage snatch and he was encouraging Bonham to take part in it ...'[He] thought he was recruiting for a robbery not for a charade.' By no stretch of the imagination was that an impossible offence to carry out and it was the offence which the appellant was inciting Bonham to commit.

Questions:

1. What does the inciter do to make him/her liable for an offence?
2. Why did Fitzmaurice's appeal fail?

Revision exercise:

TRUE OR FALSE: on inchoate offences

Below are 10 statements about the inchoate offences. In the column on the right, identify whether the statement is true or false. Spend some time considering why it is either true or false.

1	There is no common law offence of conspiracy	
2	To be liable for an attempt, it is not sufficient that I prepare for the crime; I must do something more than merely preparatory	
3	Conspiracy can still be charged even though the agreement was reached with the intended victim	
4	Incitement is triable only on indictment	
5	Although in a murder charge the intent to cause serious harm may be sufficient *mens rea*, in attempted murder, only an intention to kill is sufficient	
6	The *mens rea* of incitement is the intention that the offence incited should be carried out	
7	An offence of conspiracy is complete as soon as there is an agreement between two people that a course of action amounting to a crime should be pursued	
8	Attempt is a common-law offence	
9	There can be no conviction for conspiracy if it was impossible to carry out the crime that the parties conspired to carry out	
10	A conviction for attempt cannot occur where it was impossible to carry out the crime that the defendant allegedly attempted	

Guess the case!

Excuse me! Do you know if they sell stamps here?

POST OFFICE

POST OFFICE

POST O

Fig 16.1

17.1 Effective revision

Organising your revision

Revision may seem a painful process but you should remember the important purpose that it serves – giving you the best chance of success in the exams.

By the time you start your revision, you should have gained from your classes, from your own reading and researches, and from the homework that you have done all of the material that is essential to your exams.

Revision is not about learning anything new. Its purpose is to ensure that your knowledge and understanding of the subject go with you into the exam. So you should become absolutely familiar with what you have studied.

Following a simple checklist can help to make your revision more effective:

- Begin your revision early enough to get through everything you need to cover in a way that satisfies you that you are fully prepared for the exam.
- Have all the information you need organised and available before you start your revision programme.
- Plan a programme of revision in advance – so that you do not spend so much time on certain areas that you do not have enough time to cover everything that you need to.
- Prepare a revision timetable and checklist. You can then divide your time effectively and tick off what you have done as you go along. (In effect, I give very similar advice as this to the examiners when they are marking your exam papers, to identify in advance how many scripts they need to mark each day. It avoids them suddenly finding they need to mark three quarters of their allocation, say about 250 scripts, on the final day of marking. I am sure that you would not want that to happen.)
- Do not merely read your notes over and over again. Test yourself on a regular basis, or get someone else to test you.
- Do not overdo it, and be sure to give yourself time to relax in between.
- Use any kind of revision aids that help to make the process easier.

Creating your own revision aids

During your course you will have learned and hopefully understood a lot of detailed information on the law.

You may have very detailed notes and will inevitably use textbooks of varying lengths. What you need during your revision is first to produce and then to use much briefer, more punchy, resources.

> This can be done in different ways, as long as you end up with something that has a brief reference to all the relevant and necessary information and it is an effective memory jogger for you personally.

For instance, many students will use some form of 'key card', reducing the information to its barest form, as in the very brief example below on provocation.

PROVOCATION

s3 Homicide Act 1957– definition:
- Things said or done
- Caused D to lose self-control
- And a reasonable man would have reacted the same

Roles of judge and jury
- Judge decides whether there is provocation for jury to consider – Acott
- Jury decide whether D was provoked

The provocation
- Provocation can be things said or done, e.g. homosexual advances – Newell
- Loss of control must be temporary and sudden – Duffy
- 'Slow burn' is generally not accepted – Ahluwhalia
- And a cooling off period defeats the plea

D's characteristics
- Jury entitled to take into account characteristics of D relevant to the provocation, e.g. age, sex etc. – Camplin
- Now jury can take into account characteristics relevant to D's loss of control – Smith (Morgan James)

This example is actually carrying a lot of information and you may be able to reduce what you carry on a key card still further. There are also revision books on the market that include all of the key points in a digested form. One such series is the 'Key Facts' series by the publishers of this book. It includes titles on the English Legal System and the three main option areas at A Level: Criminal Law, Contract Law, and the Law of Torts.

You could also try to produce flow charts like the one below. They are visual, so may be less boring to revise from than notes, and they also structure the information that you need to know in a way that is also relevant to the application of that knowledge.

The remaining sections of this chapter also contain a number of different revision aids all of which I have used with students at some time during my teaching career.

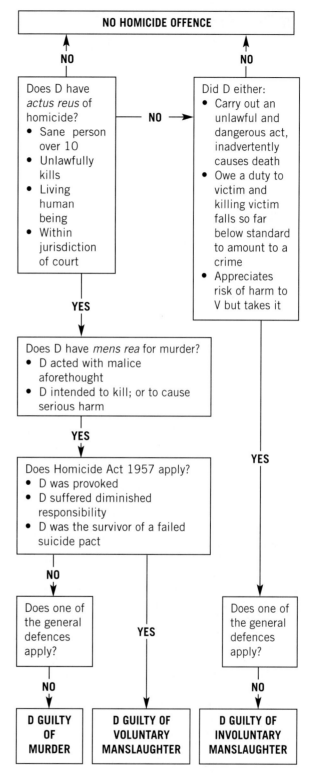

17.2 Revision aids: 20 criminal law cases

Try this as a revision aid. Below is a table containing brief facts from 20 cases, numbered 1–20. Following that is a table of 20 case names, lettered A–T. Place the number of the appropriate facts in the column next to the case name you believe that the facts apply to. In the third column, try to identify the area of criminal law from which the case comes, and briefly identify the principle of law. You could make up similar lists of your own to test yourself on specific areas.

Case facts

1	A doctor was convicted when he claimed money for an abortion that he had never carried out
2	Two striking miners were convicted when they dropped a block of concrete off a bridge into the path of a taxi carrying a working miner and the taxi driver was killed
3	A young boy killed an old man by hitting him on the head with a large frying pan after the old man had sexually abused the boy and taunted him about it
4	Two shipwrecked crew members were convicted after they killed and then ate the cabin boy in order to survive
5	A diabetic male nurse attacked and hurt one of his patients, having taken his insulin injection but having failed to eat and also having drunk alcohol. His conviction was quashed on appeal
6	A taxi driver took £6 from a foreign student for a 50p taxi ride
7	A man walked behind the till area in a department store and opened the till to see if there was any money in it
8	A man pulled on a lady's shopping bag and tried to force her to release it. When she eventually let go he dropped it as he ran off
9	A man burned down his house in order to be rehoused but his wife, girlfriend and children died in the fire and he was convicted
10	A man was convicted after making repeated silent phone calls to women at night. Some of the women suffered psychiatric harm as a result

11	The licensee of a public house failed to stop his customers from drinking up their drinks after 11.10 p.m. though licensing laws prevented drinking after this time
12	Sado-masochist homosexuals inflicted pain on each other for sexual pleasure and claimed that they should be able to do so, but their conviction was upheld
13	A company was convicted when pumps in a tank became blocked so that the tank overflowed and the escaping water polluted a river
14	A man was convicted after he stabbed a Jehovah's Witness who then died after refusing a blood transfusion
15	A man was convicted when he threw his three-month-old baby son onto a hard surface. He must have realised that what he did was virtually certain to cause serious harm to the boy
16	A man set fire to a hotel when he was very drunk and was convicted since there was an obvious risk of injury to people
17	A man was convicted when he aimed a blow at a person with a belt but hit the wrong person by mistake
18	After drinking and taking a variety of drugs over the course of a day, a man attacked both the landlord of the pub he was in and the policeman who tried to arrest him. He was convicted
19	A politician faked his own suicide by drowning in order that his wife should be able to claim insurance
20	A man was able to gain work as a self-employed accountant by telling a firm who took him on that he had qualifications that he did not in fact have

Case names

A	R v Dudley and Stephens	
B	R v Goodfellow	
C	R v Walkington	
D	Tuck v Robson	
E	R v Woollin	
F	R v Ghosh	
G	Alphacell v Woodward	
H	R v Lawrence	
I	R v Hancock and Shankland	
J	MPC v Caldwell	
K	R v Callender	
L	DPP v Majewski	
M	R v Ireland	
N	DPP v Stonehouse	
O	R v Blaue	
P	R v Clouden	
Q	R v Brown and Others	
R	R v Quick	
S	R v Latimer	
T	DPP v Camplin	

17.3 Revision aids: essential elements of offences in crime

The following are the essential ingredients of crimes on the main A Level courses. They may be a quicker revision aid than the sections of Acts or the common-law definitions themselves.

Offences against the person

Murder

1. A sane person over the age of 10
2. Unlawfully kills
3. A living human being
4. Within the jurisdiction of the English courts
5. With intent:
   (a) to kill; or
   (b) to commit GBH

Constructive manslaughter

1. A sane person over 10
2. Intentionally or recklessly
3. Does an unlawful and dangerous act
4. Which causes the death of
5. A living human being
6. Within the jurisdiction of the courts

Gross negligence manslaughter

1. A sane person over the age of 10
2. Acting under a duty
3. Does an act or omission which is so negligent as to go beyond compensation and amount to a crime
4. That causes the death of
5. A living human being
6. Within the jurisdiction of the courts

Wounding with intent – contrary to s18 Offences Against the Person Act 1861

1. Unlawfully and
2. Maliciously
3. (a) wounds; or
   (b) causes GBH
4. To any person
5. With intent to
   (a) cause GBH
   (b) resist lawful arrest

Unlawful wounding – contrary to s20 OAPA 1861

1. Unlawfully and
2. Maliciously
3. (a) wounds, or
   (b) inflicts GBH
4. On any person

Assault occasioning actual bodily harm – contrary to s47 OAPA 1861

1. Does an act (assault or battery)
2. That causes another
3. Actual bodily harm
4. With intent

    (a) to cause apprehension of immediate and unlawful violence

    (b) to cause GBH

5. Reckless as to whether

    (a) apprehension of harm is caused

    (b) actual bodily harm is caused

Common assault – s39 Criminal Justice Act 1988

1. Does an act
2. (a) Causing another apprehension of
3. immediate and unlawful violence
    (b) Inflicting violence on another
4. (a) intending to cause apprehension/inflict violence
    (b) reckless as to whether apprehension/violence is caused

Offences against property

Theft – contrary to s1 Theft Act 1968

1. Dishonestly
2. Appropriates
3. Property
4. Belonging to another
5. With the intention permanently to deprive the other of it

Robbery – contrary to s8 Theft Act 1968

1. Steals (*actus reus* and *mens rea* of theft)
2. Immediately before or at the time of the theft
3. Uses force or puts in fear of force
4. For the purpose of stealing

Burglary with intent – contrary to s9(1)(a) Theft Act 1968

1. Enters
2. A building or part of a building
3. As a trespasser
4. With intent to
    (a) steal
    (b) inflict GBH on a person therein
    (c) rape a person therein
    (d) cause criminal damage

Burglary – contrary to s9(1)(b) Theft Act 1968

1. Having entered
2. A building or part of a building
3. As a trespasser
4. (a) Steals
    (b) Inflicts GBH
    (c) Attempts either

Obtaining property by deception – contrary to s15 Theft Act 1968

1. By any deception
2. Dishonestly
3. Obtains
4. Property
5. Belonging to another
6. With the intention permanently to deprive the other of it

Obtaining services by deception – contrary to s1 Theft Act 1978

1. Dishonestly
2. Obtains services from another
3. By any deception

Evasion of liability – contrary to s2(1)(a) Theft Act 1978

1. By any deception
2. Dishonestly
3. Secures the remission of all or part of an existing debt
4. Owed by himself or by another

Evasion of liability – contrary to s2(1)(b) Theft Act 1978

1. By any deception
2. With intent to make permanent default
3. Induces a creditor to wait for payment or forego
4. A debt owed by himself or another

Evasion of liability – contrary to s2(1)(c) Theft Act 1978

1. By any deception
2. Dishonestly
3. Obtains exemption or abatement of a debt

Making off without payment – contrary to s3 Theft Act 1978

1. A person knowing payment on the spot is required
2. Dishonestly
3. Makes off without having paid as required or expected
4. Intending to avoid payment

Criminal damage – contrary to s1(1) Criminal Damage Act 1971

1. Without lawful excuse
2. Destroys or damages
3. Property
4. Belonging to another

5. (a) Intentionally
   (b) Recklessly

Recklessly endangering life – contrary to s1(2) Criminal Damage Act 1977

1. Without lawful excuse
2. Destroys or damages
3. Property
4. Belonging to himself or another
5. (a) Intentionally, or
   (b) recklessly
6. (a) Intending to endanger life, or
   (b) reckless as to whether life is endangered

Inchoate offences

Attempt – contrary to s1 Criminal Attempts Act 1981

1. With intent to commit an offence
2. Does an act
3. More than merely preparatory to the commission of the offence

Conspiracy – contrary to s1 Criminal Law Act 1977

1. Agrees
2. With another person or persons
3. To pursue a course of conduct
4. Amounting to or involving an offence
5. Intending to play a part

Incitement

1. Communicates encouragement or persuades
2. Another person
3. To commit an offence
4. Intending an offence is committed

17.4 Revision aids: essential elements of defences to crimes

The following are the essential elements of the defences studied on A Level courses. In this form they may be a quicker revision aid.

Incapacity through age (infancy)

1. Based on irrefutable presumption
2. That a child under the age of 10
3. Is incapable of forming criminal intent – so no *mens rea*

Insanity

1. Available to all crimes
2. Can mean defendant:
   (a) is incapable of pleading; or
   (b) was incapable of forming *mens rea* at time of crime
3. Based on a legal rather than a medical definition
4. Defendant is:
   (a) labouring under a defect of reasoning
   (b) caused by a disease of the mind (internal factor)
   (c) and does not know the quality of his act;
   (d) or if he does he does not know that what he did was wrong

Non-insane automatism

1. Defendant
   (a) has no voluntary actions – so is not responsible for the *actus reus*; and
   (b) is unconscious of his deeds – so has no *mens rea* either
2. So based on:
   (a) an act done without any conscious control
   (b) such as a reflex, spasm, convulsion
3. Will be caused by an external factor, e.g.
   - Concussion
   - Attack by a swarm of bees
   - Anaesthetic
   - But not sleepwalking

Intoxication

1. Covers alcohol and drugs
2. Voluntary intoxication is not a complete defence:
   (a) but can negate *mens rea* in specific intent offences, e.g. murder
   (b) but not in basic intent offences where voluntary intoxication will be recklessness
3. Involuntary intoxication:
   (a) is no defence if D had necessary *mens rea* when committing the offence
   (b) but can be a defence where D does not have the necessary *mens rea*

Consent

1. In some ways not really a defence since if the victim consents there is no offence
2. In theft, consent to appropriation does not necessarily remove liability
3. In assault, the consent means the action is not unlawful – so is common in, e.g. contact sports
4. Not generally available to wounding on public policy grounds
5. But consent to assault in a domestic context may be accepted
6. A genuinely mistaken belief in consent may be accepted

Duress

1. A 'concession to human frailty'
2. D has a defence when he committed the crime under threat of violence to himself or his family
3. But there must be a connection between the threat and the crime
4. Not available as a defence to murder, attempted murder, being an accomplice to a murder
5. Not available if D:
   - Could have escaped but did not
   - Voluntarily associated with the maker of the threats, knowing of his violent character

Duress of circumstances

1. Available as a defence if, from an objective view, the accused acted reasonably and proportionately to avoid the threats
2. Available to all crimes except murder and attempted murder
3. There must be:
   - Imminent peril of death or serious injury to death or others within D's responsibility
   - The jury must be satisfied that the threat overbore D's will at the time of committing the offence
   - Execution of the threat need not be immediate

Necessity

1. Traditionally not considered to be available for any offence
2. And this could work unfairly
3. Now linked to duress of circumstances
4. Possible now in rare cases – but only if:
   - the act is needed to avoid inevitable and irreparable evil;
   - no more is done than is reasonably necessary for the purpose to be achieved;
   - the evil inflicted is not out of proportion to the evil avoided

Mistake

1. To be a successful defence, the mistake must be one of fact, not law
2. So that if the facts were as D believed:
   - There would be no *mens rea*; or
   - D would have been unable to rely on another defence
3. The mistake need only be an honest mistake – it does not have to be reasonable
4. A drunken mistake may negative the *mens rea* of the offence

Self-defence

1. Available as a complete defence on the basis of justification

2. Can use self-defence to protect self, others or property
3. But only possible where the defendant has used reasonable force

In the case of murder, partial defences are also provided by the Homicide Act 1957 – but this merely reduces the charge to one of manslaughter, and removes the mandatory life sentence.

Diminished responsibility

1. s2 Homicide Act 1957
2. Defendant suffered from:
   - an abnormality of the mind
   - caused by:
     - arrested or retarded development of mind; or
     - any inherent causes; or
     - induced by disease or injury
     - this substantially impaired his/her mental responsibility
3. And he killed as a result

Provocation

1. s3 Homicide Act 1957
2. Defendant:
   - was provoked
   - either by things done or things said
   - so as to lose self-control
   - and kill
   - and any reasonable person
   - sharing the relevant characteristics of the defendant (i.e. that would affect the provocation or his ability to keep self-control)
   - would have reacted in the same way
3. The jury is satisfied:
   - that the defendant was provoked; and
   - that a reasonable person sharing the same relevant characteristics as the defendant would have reacted in the same way

Failed suicide pacts

1. s4 Homicide Act 1957
2. Defendant:
   - agreed with one or more people
   - to carry out a course of action that would result in their deaths
   - and the other person(s) died
   - but the defendant did not
3. The defence can satisfy the court that there was in fact a suicide pact

The nature and purpose of synoptic assessment

The synoptic element on A Level Law papers was introduced with Curriculum 2000 for first possible sitting in January 2002. In fact initially it was intended that the synoptic element should only be sat as the final A Level examination, as a result of which effective first assessment should have been in June 2002. However, QCA subsequently relaxed the rules and it can now be taken at either sitting in the A2 year.

The synoptic element was an inclusion to all A Levels insisted upon by the Dearing Report which preceded Curriculum 2000.

The general principle behind it is that candidates should be assessed in a form that demonstrates both a good overall understanding of the different components of their course, i.e. the legal system as well as the substantive area studied, and also of the ways in which the individual components connect or affect each other. So it is a general overview of the course.

Candidates choosing Criminal Law as an option on A2 would be expected to show an understanding of the way that the criminal law operates within the legal system. The individual examination boards chose different styles of papers for the synoptic element, mirroring the different emphases in their individual specifications.

AQA chose a model of synoptic assessment mirroring interest previously shown in abstract conceptual aspects of law such as justice, principles of fault, morality, etc. illustrated by use of criminal law examples (or other substantive law areas chosen as a course of study in Units 4 and 5).

OCR chose a narrower focus, basing their synoptic assessment on a previously selected theme for both legal system and substantive law elements. The theme for legal system is common for all substantive law options. A specific theme for each option is then illustrative of the central legal system theme. Building on the style of the existing Sources of Law paper,

candidates also have the support of pre-released resource materials in the exam.

WJEC chose a modular structure based on style of assessment rather than on content. For the synoptic element, a model of assessment based on a single compulsory synoptic question drawn from the AS content and an Option content were chosen.

18.2 OCR synoptic element

OCR Law examiners who prepared the draft specification for Curriculum 2000 chose to base the synoptic element, termed the Special Study, on a theme, and on use of pre-released source materials, building on use of source materials in Sources of Law.

Each theme lasts for two years or four papers.

The original theme, which lasted through the original sample materials and the January and June 2002 papers and the January 2003 papers, is 'The Law Commission and Law Reform'. Each option then has its own specific theme to go with the central theme. In the case of Criminal Law this was 'Involuntary Manslaughter'.

From June 2003 until January 2005, inclusive, the theme will be 'Precedent and the Development of Law'. The theme specific to the Criminal Law option is the linked defences of duress, duress of circumstances and necessity.

Centres are provided with booklets of source materials with which candidates can familiarise themselves during the course of their A2 year. Teachers also will be able to use the materials and the past papers to prepare candidates for the style of exam.

Candidates cannot take their original copy into the exam, but have the benefit of a clean copy of these materials in the exam room at the time of sitting the paper.

These materials are available from OCR and are usually on its web site also. They include extracts from judgments of leading cases, extracts from articles in legal journals, and extracts from better-quality text books. The questions are designed to draw on material found in these sources.

Each paper has four questions, and these are of distinct types:

Question 1

This is always a discussion of the area of the central theme (up to and including January 2003 – The Law Commission) – from June 2003 – precedent.

Questions are likely to be based on the first source in the Special Study Materials, but answers should include illustration from substantive law.

Question 2

This is always a question about a case that appears in the source materials, e.g. in June 2002 for the Criminal Law option, the theme was based on involuntary manslaughter and the case for this question was *Adomako*.

With the new theme of duress and the other associated defences, the materials include reference to cases such as *Graham, Howe, Gotts, Valderrama-Vega, Cole, Hudson and Taylor, Sharp, Shepherd, Kitson, Conway, Willer, Martin, Dudley and Stephens* and *Re A (Conjoined Twins)*. Inevitably, on any paper, Question 2 will be taken from one of these cases.

Questions will ask candidates to discuss the case in the light of the overall theme of precedent. So they may demand an understanding of how the case changed or developed the law, whether the case has restricted the law, whether the case remedies or produces injustice, etc.

Question 3

This is always the major discussion question about the substantive law theme (up to and including January 2003 – involuntary manslaughter – from June 2003 defences of duress, duress of circumstances and necessity).

Discussions under the previous theme focused on areas such as confusions in classifications of involuntary manslaughter following *Adomako*, and the advantages and disadvantages of having a law of corporate killing.

It is easy to see areas of discussion that could be asked for in relation to the three defences in the materials considering their development and the extent of their availability. Duress is not available to all offences. Duress of circumstances has been subject to an uncertain development, and necessity was thought to be unavailable.

Question 4

Always involves pure application of the area of law in the theme. This can come in the form of a small problem or as three individual scenarios. In either case, what is required is application of the principles of law appropriate to the problem. It is not the same as answering traditional problems on Paper 1 or Paper 2 of the options.

These four types of questions have specific demands relating to what is required in the exam:

Question 1

- Will always require a discussion – and may well be based on a quote from the first source.
- Candidates should be encouraged to use the source materials and illustrate by reference to them.
- Better candidates will also be supplementing information offered them in the materials by showing a wider knowledge and understanding.
- In any discussion question a balanced debate, and one that answers the question set produces the best marks.

Question 2

- Always requires a response to a case actually to be found in the materials.
- So merely reciting the facts of the case is insufficient – it requires some critical awareness of the significance of the case to the theme.
- In relation to the Law Commission theme, what was required was inevitably to do with how the case contributed to reform of the law.
- In relation to the precedent theme from June 2003, what is required is reference back to the precedent context in which the question will be set.

Question 3

- Always requires a discussion about the substantive area – but candidates should not forget the overall theme of precedent and the development of law.

- Again, the source material will be relevant and should be used.
- The question may ask, e.g., for a criticism of how the defence has developed.
- Or it may refer to a quote from a source from either an author or a judge in an extract from a judgment and then require comment on the quote.

Question 4

- This always calls for pure application of law to be found in the source materials.
- Again, it is the understanding of the principles through application that is important, rather than regurgitating facts.
- Candidates have already scored high marks on this question by employing the skills learned on the 'Sources of Law' paper.

Below are examples of these types of questions taken from past papers or from the specimen paper submitted to QCA. They refer to the previous Law Commission/involuntary manslaughter theme, but the style of question could be applied to the precedent/duress defences theme to get an idea of what is required:

Example question 1:

The Law Commission recommends changes to the criminal law in its 1996 Report: 'Legislating The Code – Involuntary Manslaughter'.

Critically consider the role of the Law Commission in assisting Parliament to change the law. **[Specimen paper]**

Example question 2:

Explain the effects of the judgment in *Adomako* on the law of manslaughter. **[June 2002]**

Example question 3:

How satisfactory is it that there are only **two** different ways, (constructive manslaughter and gross negligence manslaughter), by which involuntary manslaughter can be committed? **[January 2002]**

Example question 4:

Den is the landlord of a public house. One evening after closing time his 15-year-old daughter and her 16-year-old boyfriend Tom enter the pub. Tom asks Den if he will sell him a bottle of vodka, which he says he is going to drink in one go for a bet he has with Emily. Den initially explains to Tom that he cannot serve him but then agrees and sells the vodka to Tom. Tom then does quickly drink all of the contents of the bottle, and falls into a chair in a drunken state. Den then goes into the private living quarters and goes to bed. During the night Tom dies from alcohol poisoning.

Consider the criminal liability of Den under the law of manslaughter. **[June 2002]**

18.3 AQA synoptic element

For the synoptic unit, candidates sitting AQA Unit 6: Concepts of Law are expected to use material in illustration of their answers from anywhere in the other five units.

In order to demonstrate a synthesis of their understanding of legal processes and institutions as well as the substantive areas of law studied, candidates are asked to answer questions on a number of conceptual areas.

These concepts of law are:

- The law and morals
- The law and justice
- The balancing of conflicting interests
- The principle of fault
- Judicial creativity

Even a very brief examination of these broad headings can hint at fairly obvious areas of interest in a study of criminal law:

- Criminal law inevitably involves moral judgments even if individual crimes do not always represent the most common moral standpoints.
- Criminal law is inevitably seeking justice for the victim of crime through punishment of the criminal.
- Not so much with the substantive areas of crime, but certainly sentencing policy is all about the competing interests of the victim, the state and also the criminal in terms of his/her rehabilitation and fair and proportionate treatment.
- Fault is an ever-present concept in crime, criminal intent being required for all but strict liability crimes.
- Judges say that they only declare the law, not make it. But a brief glance at the history of intention in

murder or the rectification of a mistaken interpretation of law in criminal attempts seem to suggest that judges can be quite creative. Judges also play a major role.

In answering questions on these concepts, candidates will need to demonstrate understanding of the concepts themselves:

In the case of law and morality:

- Questions here will involve exploring the distinction between the two, e.g. that morals depend on voluntary codes while legal rules are enforceable in the courts; that morality can have a social context and develops over time, where legal rules can be introduced instantly without reference to popular views; that things included in a moral code do not always appear in legal rules; and that some things that are accepted in law may still offend some people's sense of morality, e.g. abortion.
- It will inevitably involve exploring the Hart/Devlin debate, i.e. between the views that morality is a private concept and that the law should not intervene in a person's private morality, and the view that judges have an inherent right to protect the public from moral lapses.
- Some context will be introduced to illustrate whether law and morals do coincide – it is reasonably easy in criminal law where there are numerous sexual offences, and also where there is control over things such as euthanasia.

In the case of law and justice:

- Questions will involve some discussion of individual theories of justice and explanations of the theories of natural lawyers, positivists, the utilitarian theories of Bentham and John Stuart Mill, as well as Marxist theorists could all be explored.
- Problems that surface here obviously include the fact that what is just for society as a whole may be unjust to the individual and *vice versa*.
- The fact that unjust laws are possible can also be considered, e.g. when looking at cases such as *Ahluwalia* it is possible to argue that provocation is very much a male defence.
- Ways of achieving justice should also be considered – obvious examples here are the fact that crimes are graded according to various things including perceived wickedness, and this is reflected in the sentences available.

In the case of balancing conflicting interests:

- Again, questions here will focus on the extent to which individual rights can be protected as against the interests of the state or indeed competing interests.
- In criminal law this is often a question of looking at the extent to which victims can be satisfied that justice has been served while factors like standard of proof are used to ensure that an accused is fairly treated and sentencing policy is used to ensure that perpetrators of different crimes are treated proportionately.

In the case of the principle of liability based on fault:

- Questions here would demand an understanding of fault, i.e. that liability should depend on culpability and responsibility.
- The fact that criminal law depends on proof of *mens rea* is an obvious illustration of fault.
- Interesting features are the different ways in which fault is shown, i.e. full-blown intent, subjective and objective recklessness and gross negligence.
- By contrast, crimes of strict liability can be considered and the restrictions placed on them by judges.

In the case of judicial creativity:

- Questions will inevitably involve an explanation of the restrictions on judicial creativity, i.e. Parliament is the supreme law-maker, judges adhere to a declaratory theory of law, a rigid doctrine of precedent.
- Means of avoiding this would also be considered, e.g. any flexibility within the doctrine of precedent including the Practice Statement 1966, the impact that judges can have on legislation through statutory interpretation, and processes like judicial review.
- In illustration, reference could be made to areas that have been principally developed by the common law, e.g. murder and in particular the definition of intention; the rules on the applicability of individual defences, e.g. duress.

Examples of questions include:

1. Discuss the meaning of 'justice'. Consider the extent to which justice is achieved in the application of legal rules. Relate your answer to examples drawn from civil law, criminal law or both.

2. Discuss the relationship between law and morals. Consider how far the law seeks to uphold and promote moral values.

[Questions 3 and 4 from June 2002]

The following three sections are an indication of what is required in an examination question:
- in essay form (Section 19.1),
- as a problem (Section 19.2),
- in data response or source-based questions (Section 19.3).

They are not the answers themselves, although they do incorporate the elements of answering each of the three different types of question in turn. They are rather a structure, a way of identifying what needs to be done in any law exam in response to the particular style of questioning. In that sense the process can be repeated mentally or in very brief note form when considering the essential ingredients of the question set prior to writing the actual answer.

Remember, any brief moments spent planning actually save time in the long run.

Writing an essay on criminal law

Answering an essay question

When candidates had the choice of completing more essays than problems in an exam, they frequently did so. This may mean that essay questions are seen as being easier in comparison with problems but in fact they are not. It is true that in most cases you are told in the question what the specific area of law is that the examiner wishes you to write about. Nevertheless, if you are trying to gain good marks, finding out what the subject-matter of the essay is helps with only one part of actually answering it. It is very tempting to see that the essay is, for instance, about involuntary manslaughter and then to use your memory of your lecture notes and repeat everything that was there on involuntary manslaughter. However, as an experienced examiner, I have never known a colleague to prepare an exam question entitled 'Write all you know about involuntary manslaughter' and I doubt you have seen such a question either. Similarly, I have never known a colleague to write an essay title 'Write the answer to the question on involuntary manslaughter from last year's paper'. However, as examiners, we often see candidates' work that falls into that trap. There is nothing wrong with learning how to write essays by using acceptable answers to past questions. However, even if they do appear again it will not be at the very next sitting, so rote learning a model answer to last year's question is really not productive. It is much better to have a full understanding of the area itself, and to appreciate the kinds of questions that can be asked.

The important thing is to try to answer the question set. So if the question asks you to 'Consider the difficulties faced by the courts in establishing what is an unlawful act for the purposes of constructive manslaughter' there is no point in discussing gross negligence manslaughter in too much detail. Although gross negligence will appear in your notes on involuntary manslaughter, it is of no relevance to the question and if you include it you are only taking up time that you could better use on your next question.

The title considered below is rather broader in content than you may usually see.

Most essay questions that are set contain at least two elements:

- A requirement for you to display factual knowledge – so it is important to stick to relevant details only and not to stray into the irrelevant. This merely makes the examiner think that you are throwing in your entire knowledge on an area indiscriminately, to impress with the breadth of your knowledge. In fact it has the opposite effect. It is important also not to assume knowledge on the part of the examiner, so define all terminology. Also, the factor that will distinguish your essay from someone who has not studied law is the extent to which it is supported by the case law and statute.

- A critical element – most essays do not merely test knowledge but also your appreciation of it. This is why words like 'discuss' and 'evaluate', and other similar terms are used. This is often the crux of an essay question. The extent to which you appreciate how the law is inadequate, or why it is complicated or inconsistent is tested here. So you should at least try to respond to the particular question asked and direct your knowledge towards that point. Again, the most effective essay answers contain some sort of considered argument and reach some kind of conclusion. Reading the types of articles from which extracts in this book are taken is a good way of developing a critical awareness and of finding good arguments to use in essay questions.

Essay title:

Consider the extent to which judges have struggled to develop satisfactory definitions for the different types of involuntary manslaughter.

Knowledge

1. It is clearly important to start by defining involuntary manslaughter – in other words, an unlawful killing without malice aforethought, and so not murder – and also the partial defences for voluntary manslaughter do not apply.
2. The *actus reus* can be identified as that for all homicides: the unlawful killing by a sane person over the age of 10 of a reasonable living human being within the jurisdiction of the English courts.
3. Then it will be necessary to identify and define the different forms of involuntary manslaughter:
4. Constructive manslaughter:
   • Requires an unlawful act (rather than a lawful act carried out unlawfully): *Andrews v DPP*
   • The act must be dangerous, objectively measured: *Church*
   • There must be an inadvertent death caused by the unlawful act
   • *Mens rea* is that for the unlawful act: *DPP v Newbury & Jones*
   • There is no requirement that the unlawful act should be directed at the victim: *Goodfellow*
5. Gross negligence manslaughter:
   • Based on existence of a duty of care owed to victim, breach of duty by the defendant, causing death of victim
   • In addition the jury must decide whether the defendant's behaviour in the circumstances falls so far below the appropriate standard as to amount to a crime: *Bateman*
   • So goes well below mere compensation *Andrews: v DPP*
   • And arises in duties voluntarily undertaken: *Stone and Dobinson*
   • Or arising from specific relationships, e.g. doctor/patient: *Adomako*
6. Recklessness:
   • *Lidar* has recently accepted the possibility of reckless manslaughter
   • This would be measured subjectively – defendant appreciated the existence of the risk and nevertheless carried on to take it

(Cunningham) – so confirms the retreat from *Seymour* in *Adomako*
7. Without using great detail, it might be appropriate briefly to distinguish involuntary manslaughter from murder: requiring malice aforethought – intention to kill or cause serious harm; and from voluntary manslaughter –unlawful killing with malice aforethought but defendant either suffered diminished responsibility, was provoked; or was the survivor of a failed suicide pact
8. In light of the potential critical comment for this essay some appreciation could also be shown of the Law Commission's proposed reforms by the introduction of offences of reckless killing, and killing by gross carelessness

Critical comment

1. The essay is really asking for two things:
   • some form of critical account of the development of the definitions of the various types of involuntary manslaughter.
   • an evaluation of the extent to which they leave the law in a satisfactory state.
2. We have already identified above the wide range of factual information that is appropriate in this essay, charting the development of the different types of involuntary manslaughter – and in doing so critical comments should be added both in relation to the area in general and in relation to the specific types.
3. Critical comment on involuntary manslaughter in general could include:
   • that the area is excessively broad, including all levels of unlawful killing, from a killing which is slightly more than accidental to a killing which falls just short of murder – and that only sentencing then distinguishes one from the other
   • that the area generally lacks any clear or obvious structure and there is little or no cohesion between the different types of involuntary manslaughter
   • there could be uncertainty in determining which type should be charged, e.g. see the drugs-related cases of *Cato, Dalby* etc.
   • there is some inconsistency of approach regarding omissions, e.g. see *Lowe*
   • at least prior to *Lidar* there was the possibility that certain killings might not fall under any category
   • because following *Adomako* there was uncertainty regarding the actual categories of unlawful manslaughter.
4. Critical comment on constructive manslaughter might include:
   • that it is potentially unfair because the focus is more on the unlawful act than the killing
   • the fact that the defendant may be convicted in circumstances where death may never have been foreseen

- the difficulties of showing the unlawful: act *Andrews, Dalby* etc.
5. Critical comment on gross negligence manslaughter might include:
   - the 'circularity' of the test
   - the role of the jury
   - the confusion with civil law principles
   - the problem of defining how far below the standard the defendant must fall
   - but this type obviously more easily accommodates liability for omissions.
6. Critical comment on reckless manslaughter might include:
   - the reasons why HL in *Adomako* rejected *Seymour* and *Lawrence*
   - that even before *Lidar* many commentators saw a need to retain subjective recklessness, as in *Pike*.

Conclusions

The best facts will draw all of this factual knowledge and critical comment to some form of conclusion.
- The logical one to make here is to accept that the courts have had difficulty in defining different types of involuntary manslaughter, and in fact have moved through contrary positions at times.
- Also the fact that some of the Law Commission's criticisms and proposals could be referred to
- This in itself may be seen as justifying the criticism in the quote – but any attempt to agree or disagree with the quote is acceptable providing that it has been reasonably supported by argument.

19.2 Answering a problem question on criminal law

Answering a problem question

Problem questions may seem hard at first because the first thing that you have to do is to decide what the problem is all about and what area of the law is being tested, unlike in an essay where you are told this.

There is always certain information in any problem question that will lead you to the specific area of law. If you look back over past exam papers you will find that the same type of information will always be given for the specific area of law. So it becomes easier to recognise the issues and deal with them the more used you are to seeing the problems.

There are always four essential ingredients to answering problem questions:

- First, you must be able to identify which are the key facts in the problem; those on which resolution of the problem depends.
- Second, you will need to identify which is the appropriate law applying to the particular situation in the problem.
- Third, you must apply the law to the facts.
- Finally, you will need to reach conclusions of some sort. If the question asks you to advise, then that is what you need to do. (Advice is something that a client would need in deciding whether to defend the charges and how, so your advice must be capable of leading to that decision.) On the other hand, if the problem says 'Discuss the legal consequences of …' then you know that you can be less positive in your conclusions.

Problem scenario:

Florence has an argument with her husband Andy and storms out of their house. As she goes, in a temper, she kicks her next-door neighbour's fence, causing it to shatter. One of the dislodged fencing poles flies up, hitting Florence on the head and leaving her dazed and confused. Giles, Florence's next-door neighbour, comes out from his house to see what has happened. Florence picks up the fencing pole and hits Giles hard on the arm, causing it to bleed. Andy runs out of the house and tries to stop Florence, who hits him on the head with the fencing pole, causing him to lose consciousness.

Giles and Andy are both taken to hospital and treated by Dr Dodgy. Giles has only slight cuts and bruises and his treatment is straightforward. Andy's head injuries are very serious and he is placed in an intensive care unit. Dr Dodgy forgets to ask whether Andy is allergic to any drugs and injects Andy with antibiotics. In fact, Andy is allergic to antibiotics, has a bad reaction to the drugs and dies soon afterwards.

The facts

It is always important to have a clear idea of what the principal facts are. Here there are only four characters and the scenario is not excessively complex. However, sometimes problem questions contain a number of different people and a variety of individual problems are involved.

The main facts here appear to be:

1. Florence (F) argues with her husband Andy (A) and storms out of the house in a temper.
2. F kicks her next-door neighbour's (Giles's) (G) fence so hard that it breaks.
3. A wooden pole from the fence hits F on the head, leaving her dazed and confused.
4. G comes out to investigate.
5. F hits J on the arm, breaking the skin.
6. A comes out to stop F who hits him on the head, leaving him unconscious.
7. G and A are taken to hospital and treated by Dr Dodgy (D).
8. G's injuries are slight.
9. A's head injuries are serious.
10. D forgets to ask if A has any allergies.
11. D gives A antibiotics.
12. A is allergic to the drug and dies.

The appropriate law

From your appreciation of the different factual elements you should be able to work out the various offences indicated in the problem, any potential defences, or other legal principles that are important in resolving the issues.

Here they would most likely involve:

1. Criminal damage:
   - s1(1) Criminal Damage Act 1971
   - *Mens rea* = intention or recklessness (*Caldwell* objective type – obvious risk)
   - *Actus reus* = destroys or damages property belonging to another (requires some impairment of value or some cost, e.g. compare *Roe* v *Kingerlee* with *A* (*a minor*))
2. Assault occasioning actual bodily harm:
   - s47 Offences against the Person Act 1861
   - *Mens rea* = intention or recklessness (*Cunningham* subjective type – appreciates a risk but carries on to take it – *Parmenter, Savage, Spratt* in the context of assaults or wounding)
   - *Actus reus* = assault (including battery) plus some actual harm – *Venna* – bruising may be sufficient
3. Malicious wounding:
   - s20 Offences Against the Person Act 1861
   - *Mens rea* = malice, which here means intention or recklessness (as for s47)
   - *Actus reus* = wounds or inflicts GBH (wounding requires a breaking of both dermis and epidermis – *JCC* v *Eisenhower*)
4. Constructive manslaughter:
   - *Actus reus* = same as for murder: sane person over 10 unlawfully kills another living human being residing under the Queen's Peace
   - *Mens rea* = same as for unlawful act
   - Requires unlawful act rather than lawful act carried out unlawfully: *Andrews* v *DPP*
   - Act must be objectively dangerous: *Church*
   - And death inadvertently occurs
   - But unlawful act need not be directed at victim: *Goodfellow*
5. Causation:
   - Important in 'result' crimes
   - D must be factual cause of outcome: *White*
   - And legal cause of outcome: *Pagett*
   - Medical negligence only breaks chain of causation if has become the sole cause of the outcome – compare *Jordan* with *Smith* and *Cheshire*
6. Non-insane automatism:
   - Complete defence – no voluntary conduct – so no *actus reus* – D unconscious and incapable of forming intent – so no *mens rea*
   - Definition in *Bratty* – involuntary act without any control of the mind – spasm, reflex, concussion
   - So based on external factor
   - Not available to crimes of basic intent if self-induced

Applying the law to the facts

1. F kicking and breaking the fence:
   - *Caldwell* recklessness only requires an obvious risk of damage – it would not matter if F had not intended to damage the fence
   - F has kicked the fence hard enough for it to shatter – this could be damage or destruction
   - There is an obvious cost here in repairing the fence
2. F hitting G with the fencing pole – G's cuts and bruises:
   - There is an assault
   - The injuries are sufficient to amount to actual harm
   - The whole skin is broken – so there could be wounding
   - Problem may be showing *mens rea*
3. F hitting A – A's head injuries and death:
   - It may be possible to argue murder – but it is easier to apply unlawful act manslaughter in the circumstances
   - There is an assault for unlawful act
   - Hitting someone on the head with a pole is objectively dangerous
   - Again, the *mens rea* may be problematic
4. D's negligence and causation:
   - Andy has suffered serious injuries – the question is whether or not they are likely to lead to death
   - Dodgy has clearly been negligent
   - F will still be liable unless on the facts *Jordan* can apply – medical negligence the sole cause of death

5. F's dazed, confused state – automatism:
   - F has suffered an external cause of a temporary mental condition
   - The question is whether she is completely unaware of her actions.

Conclusions

1. F clearly liable for damage to the fence
2. Whether or not F is liable for the injuries to G depends on her ability to claim non-insane automatism – if she can, she has a complete defence
3. If A's injuries were sufficiently serious that D's negligence is not the sole cause of death then there is no break in the chain of causation from F's actions
4. Whether F is liable for A's death depends on her ability to claim non-insane automatism – which may give her a complete defence – unless kicking the fence is then seen as constituting self-induced automatism

19.3 Answering data response questions on criminal law

What follows is an indication of what is required in an examination question where you are given source material to read and on which the questions are based. It is not the answer to the questions, although it incorporates the elements of answering the question. It is rather a structure, a way of identifying what needs to be done in any question based on source material. In that sense the process can be repeated mentally or in very brief note form when considering the essential ingredients of responding to the information contained in the source and to the questions set on it prior to writing the actual answers.

Answering source-based question papers

Source-based questions are not new. They have been common in a number of subjects, like History, for a long time. They have also been around in Law, at GCSE. Sources are not sufficient in themselves to answer the question, so you will need to bring both knowledge and understanding into the exam as well as being given the source material.

However, as with problems, the source can provide a great deal of information necessary to answer the questions, and indeed will lead you anyway to specific areas of law, and even specific problem areas to do with the law in the source material. You are given

reading time with source-based questions, even if this only appears on the front of the paper as 'including reading time' without saying that a specific period of time is to be set aside to read the source material. You should make use of this reading time then to familiarise yourself with the source material. It is a good idea to get used to identifying important issues that crop up within the source. With practice in doing this you will find not only that there are elements in the source that can be used or referred to in your answers, but also that you are probably able to guess what types of questions are coming up even before you have read them, just by reading the source material.

It is in the nature of using source material that an examiner is able then to use the material to ask you a variety of different types of questions:

- You can be asked questions specifically testing your knowledge of a given area.
- You could be asked to consider a problem area identified in the source and to analyse, or discuss, or comment, or evaluate, as you might have been called on to do in essay-type questions.
- You might also be asked to apply material found in the source, which is fairly similar to what you may come across in traditional problem questions.

You should be prepared, therefore, to be able to answer in all of these different ways. One advantage of this is that you get the opportunity to use the skills that you are good at as well as those where you may have less confidence.

Source material:

Extract adapted from 'Manslaughter: *Dalby* Revisited', Stephen O'Doherty, *Justice of the Peace*, Vol. 163, 8/5/1999, pp 368–371

The offence of manslaughter can be divided into two limbs: voluntary and involuntary. The latter may itself be divided into two further categories: causing death by an unlawful and dangerous act and causing death by an act of gross negligence while a duty of care exists. This article concentrates upon the 'unlawful act' limb of the offence and its relationship to s23 Offences Against the Persons Act 1861.

The material parts of s23 provide that 'whosoever shall unlawfully and maliciously administer to, or cause to be administered to or taken by any other person any poison or other destructive or noxious thing, so as to endanger the life of such person ... shall be guilty of an offence.'

In *Cato,* the appellant went with friends back to the house they shared. One of them named Farmer produced a bag of heroin and syringes. Farmer and Cato each filled up the syringe with the amount of heroin he wished and then gave the syringe to the other to inject him. The strength of the mixture was determined by the person who was going to receive it. Farmer died and Cato was charged with manslaughter and administering a noxious thing contrary to s23.

The appeal centred on unlawful act manslaughter. Lord Widgery CJ dealt with the act of injecting the heroin. 'It may seem strange to most of us, although possession or supply of heroin is an offence, it is not an offence to take it or to administer it.' The fact that heroin was a noxious thing was sufficient to dismiss the appeal against the conviction for the s23 offence. In the view of the court the prohibition in that statute therefore made the injection of heroin into another an unlawful act for the purposes of the offence of manslaughter. In this case it would seem that the court was extending the accused's initial criminal act of possession and supply so that the entire incident, including the injection, thereby became unlawful.

In *Dalby* somewhat different circumstances arose. The defendant supplied Diconal, a class A drug, which he lawfully possessed, to the deceased, O'Such. Each prepared the tablets and then injected the drugs into himself. The following day O'Such was found dead from the effects of the drugs. Dalby pleaded guilty to supplying drugs and was convicted of manslaughter. The Court of Appeal quashed the manslaughter conviction, holding that the act of supplying a controlled drug was not an act which caused direct harm. The defendant had committed an unlawful act with supplying the drugs but the unlawful act had stopped with the supply. It had not caused O'Such's death. There was no s23 offence for the prosecution to rely on for the unlawful act because Dalby had not administered the drug.

In July 1998 the Court of Appeal had the opportunity to consider a case where the facts fell between those in *Cato* and *Dalby*. The deceased, Bosque, asked the accused for drugs. Kennedy agreed, prepared a syringe with a heroin mixture, handed the syringe to Bosque who immediately injected himself. A short time later Bosque stopped breathing and was subsequently pronounced dead. Kennedy was prosecuted for supplying heroin and for manslaughter based on the commission of an unlawful and dangerous act. In *Cato* the deceased determined the strength of the mixture but it was

actually administered by the accused, hence the count under s23. In *Dalby*, the drugs were supplied by the defendant but it was the deceased who actually made up the mixture and injected himself. The principal distinction in *Kennedy* was the act of filling the syringe with the mixture. However the court declined to follow *Dalby* and applied *Cato*. Waller LJ stated: 'The injection of the heroin by Bosque was itself an unlawful act and if the appellant assisted in and wilfully encouraged that unlawful conduct he would himself be acting unlawfully.'

The basis of the decision therefore seems to be that the act of injection of a noxious thing by Bosque was itself unlawful and thereby Kennedy aided and abetted that unlawful act. The offence committed by Bosque was possession and that offence was completed at the moment he took the syringe from Kennedy. The act of injecting it added nothing to that offence. It is respectfully submitted that to infer that the self-injection itself was a separate criminal act is incorrect.

One aspect which has not yet been dealt with in detail is the central requirement that there must be an 'unlawful act'. Lord Widgery [in *Cato*] viewed the entire incident as a whole but it is necessary to be able to identify the precise unlawful act in order to ascertain if an act which might be unsavoury is an unlawful act for these purposes. As the actual *consumption* of heroin is not, of itself, illegal, is the act of injection an unlawful act? It seems clear from *Cato* that the court did not consider the act of injection illegal *per se* although it appears that the court in *Kennedy* came to a different conclusion.

It is submitted that on its own facts, the conviction of *Kennedy* can (just) be upheld. It was not the supply of the heroin which justified the conviction for manslaughter, but that Kennedy's actions caused Bosque to take the noxious substance which was responsible for his death.

Questions:

(a) Lines 1 and 2 of the source refer to 'voluntary manslaughter' and 'involuntary manslaughter'. Briefly outline the differences between the two.
(b) Using the source and decided cases, critically discuss the offence of 'constructive' or 'unlawful act' manslaughter.
(c) Giving reasons, consider whether any of the following are likely to be prosecuted for constructive manslaughter in the light of the three cases in the source and other cases:

(i) Amanda and Rachel went together to Rachel's house where Amanda produced a tin of solvent-based glue. They put some glue in a carrier bag and both began sniffing the glue in turn. When Rachel was barely conscious she asked Amanda to put more glue in the bag and for Amanda to put the bag over her (Rachel's) nose. Some time later, Rachel fell unconscious and died.

(ii) George asked Ronald, the landlord of a pub, to sell him two bottles of whisky to take home when it was after hours. Ronald sold George the whisky. Ronald drank both bottles in a short space of time when he got home and later died.

(iii) Jaz, who was depressed, asked Simon to supply him with amphetamines. While Simon was still with him Jaz took a fatal dose of the pills. Later, after Simon had left, Jaz died.

Before you answer any of the three questions, you can identify certain things in the source itself:

1. There is reference to involuntary manslaughter right from the start, so there is a fair chance you will be asked something about it.
2. In particular, the source focuses on 'constructive' or 'unlawful act' manslaughter, so you know that this will be a basis for questioning.
3. Much of the source material is considering what will and will not amount to an unlawful act for the purposes of a manslaughter charge, so that it is likely that this will be a focus for questions too.
4. Finally, the source is also about deaths caused by using drugs and administering noxious substances, so this element will probably be there in the questions too.

Answering Question (a)

The first question is predominantly knowledge based; some of it you can find from the source material as there is some information on what amounts to 'involuntary manslaughter' in the source itself. The details on voluntary manslaughter you will need to provide yourself.

Also, you should remember that the question says 'briefly', so there is no need to give a blow-by-blow account of every last detail of every element of the offences.

So your answer could include that:

- All forms of manslaughter share the same *actus reus* as for murder: the unlawful killing of a living

human being by a sane person over the age of 10 within the jurisdiction of the English courts.

- Voluntary manslaughter occurs where it is possible to show not only this *actus reus* but also the *mens rea* for murder: malice aforethought, to whereas with involuntary manslaughter malice aforethought, the intent to kill or to cause grievous, that is serious, bodily harm, cannot be shown.
- With voluntary manslaughter the prosecution will therefore have brought a charge of murder whereas with involuntary manslaughter it may not.
- With voluntary manslaughter the defendant will ask for the court to accept one of three pleas from the Homicide Act 1957: diminished responsibility under s2, provocation under s3, or a failed suicide pact under s4, and will do so in order to reduce the charge and avoid a mandatory life sentence.
- In the case of involuntary manslaughter the defendant will be able to show insufficient *mens rea* for murder and the prosecution will involve either the commission of an unlawful act which is recognised as dangerous and which inadvertently causes death (constructive), or a death caused where the defendant, who owes a duty of care to the victim, falls so far below the appropriate standard that it goes beyond compensation and amounts to a crime, or indeed a death caused by recklessness, where an unjustified risk of harm has been recognised but nevertheless been taken.

Answering Question (b)

The question asks you to 'critically discuss' the offence, and also to use cases and the source – so you should use cases in illustration of your explanation of the offence, and also include some sort of critical comment.

Your factual ingredients might include:

- An explanation that unlawful act manslaughter involves an unlawful act, which is dangerous, and which causes the inadvertent death of the victim.
- That the *actus reus* will therefore be the same as for all homicides.
- That the *mens rea* will be the same as for the unlawful act.
- That the act must be unlawful rather than a lawful act carried out unlawfully; and use *Andrews v DPP*.
- That the act must be such that all sober and reasonable people would recognise that it would subject the other to at least the risk of some harm; and use cases such as *R v Church* and *DPP v Newbury and Jones*.
- That although, according to *Dawson*, traditionally the unlawful act had to be directed towards the victim, following *Goodfellow* this no longer seems to be the case.

- That lawful justification for the act may mean it is not unlawful: *R v Scarlett*

Your critical comments might include:

- That the offence is difficult to prove.
- That in some circumstances it can seem unfair that a person should be guilty of a homicide offence because they did an unlawful and dangerous act.
- The problem in *Cato* of what actually amounts to an unlawful act, and whether the definition of unlawful act is sometimes stretched too far.
- That the Law Commission has criticised the offence in numerous ways:
  - the uncertainty of circumstances where omission can lead to liability
  - the sheer breadth of circumstances leading to the offence
  - the difficulty of applying sentences
  - that the offence is unprincipled because it 'requires only a foreseeable risk of some harm' and has suggested reform of the law.

Answering Question (c)

You should be aware that when using application questions the examiner will try to use the source, material to steer you towards the answers, so they will be based on the law that emerges from the source. Sometimes the scenarios that the examiner creates will be distinguishable from the cases in the source, and sometimes not. Here you should be able to recognise that the three scenarios in Question (c) are based in turn on each of the three cases in the source: *Cato*, *Dalby* and *Kennedy*.

(i) In the case of Amanda you would identify that, as in *Cato*, it was the administering of the noxious thing, the glue, that can be classed as the unlawful act under s23, with the resultant death being manslaughter because of this. But you should also note the similarities with *Khan and Khan* and consider the attitudes of the judges in that case to the applicability of gross negligence manslaughter, and whether a duty of care exists in this situation.

(ii) In the case of Ronald you will recognise that *Dalby* applies. Though Ronald has engaged in an unlawful act, the selling of the whisky after hours, this in itself is not dangerous, and so cannot be the cause of the death.

(iii)Simon's case seems to reproduce some of the complexities of *Kennedy*. His unlawful act is the supplying of an illegal drug but this has no connection with the death of Jaz. It is Simon's aiding and abetting of Jaz's offence that puts him in danger of a manslaughter charge. Since he handed the pills to Jaz, knew he was depressed and saw Jaz take so many of the pills, this may amount to the 'wilful encouragement' identified in the

article. You should also be aware of the case of *Dias*, and the reactions of the Court of Appeal in that case to *Kennedy*.